RECLAIMING
STOLEN INTIMACY

When Your Marriage is
INVADED BY PORNOGRAPHY

PICKING UP
THE PIECES

BY RENEE AND CLAY CROSSE WITH BEN COLTER

✛ LifeWay
Biblical Solutions for Life

Reclaiming Stolen Intimacy: When Your Marriage is Invaded by Pornography
© 2008 Renee and Clay Crosse

Published by Serendipity House Publishers
Nashville, Tennessee

ISBN: 978-1-5749-4423-5
Item Number: 005126278

Scripture quotations marked HCSB taken from the Holman Christian Standard Bible®, Copyright © 1999, 2000, 2002, 2003 by Holman Bible Publishers. Used by permission.

Scriptures marked NIV taken from the Holy Bible, New International Version, Copyright © 1973, 1978, 1984 by International Bible Society. Used by permission.

Scriptures marked NLT taken from the The Holy Bible, New Living Translation, Copyright © 1996, 2004. Used by permission of Tyndale House Publishers, Inc. Carol Stream, IL 60189. All rights reserved.

Scriptures marked NASB from the New American Standard Bible®, © 1960, 1962, 1963, 1968, 1971, 1972, 1973, 1975, 1977, 1995 by the Lockman Foundation. Used by permission.

Scriptures marked ESV taken from The Holy Bible, English Standard, Copyright © 2001 by Crossway Bibles, a publishing ministry of Good News Publishers. Used by permission. All rights reserved.

Scriptures marked The Message taken from the THE MESSAGE, Copyright © 1993, 1994, 1995, 1996, 2000, 2001, 2002. Used by permission of NavPress Publishing Group.

To purchase additional copies of this resource or other studies:
ORDER ONLINE at www.SerendipityHouse.com;
WRITE Serendipity by LifeWay, One LifeWay Plaza, Nashville, TN 37234
FAX (615) 277-8181

1-800-458-2772
www.SerendipityHouse.com

Printed in the United States of America
14 13 12 11 10 09 08   1 2 3 4 5 6 7 8 9 10

CONTENTS

PICKING UP THE PIECES RESOURCES

REAL HELP FOR REAL PEOPLE LIVING REAL LIFE.

How do we make sense of the times of pain and suffering in our lives? How can we reconcile the reality of our pain with the goodness of God?

Whenever you struggle, God's heart aches for you. He desperately wants to walk with you through the difficult and desperate times of your life so He can lead you to hope, healing, and freedom. Picking Up the Pieces is a series of honest, experiential Bible studies that will help you along the unfamiliar journey of rediscovering your heart!

- Written by leading therapists from the American Association of Christian Counselors
- Honest, experiential Bible studies that will set captives free from destructive patterns
- Probing questions for your heart and for God to help bind up the broken places
- Unique journaling experiences at the end of each session
- Replaces beauty for ashes and glory for shame

GREAT RESOURCES FOR:

- Support Groups
- Small Groups
- Accountability Groups
- Recovery Groups
- Church Classes and Soul Care Ministries
- Counseling Centers

Reclaiming Stolen Intimacy
When Your Marriage is Invaded by Pornography

Your home is not immune. Every Christian man in our X-rated society faces the constant challenge to remain sexually pure. The temptation from Internet pornography is only a mouse-click away. This eight-session study helps women, no matter how long they've been married or dating, to know how to compassionately but firmly deal with this tragedy. *Reclaiming Stolen Intimacy* will help women address their own personal emotional responses as well as relational issues in the rebuilding process.

"Is there something wrong with me?" "How can he really love me?" "Why did he go elsewhere for sexual satisfaction?" Every feeling you're experiencing is valid—anger, hurt, disappointment, resentment, and fear. Don't discount those feelings because they're real. But you can add something new today to what you're feeling: HOPE.

During the difficult and painful times, more than anything we need to hear personally from God. We cry out to God when we realize that we cannot "fix" the situations in which we find ourselves. He longs for you to invite Him into your pain. God is at work; He will not abandon you. He promises to redeem the worst messes of your life!

You must recognize the real enemy who wants to destroy your husband, your security, your family, and your witness to a broken world. Learn to engage in the fierce battle for husband and your marriage. Gone are the simple, nice prayers of polite Christianity. Gone are the short, pat answers to our problems.

When you forgive, you allow God to work in your life and in your husband's life. When you give a blessing instead of retaliating, you see the power of God unleashed. When you honestly share your feelings with gentleness, love, and respect, your husband won't know what hit him ... because eventually you'll touch his heart.

Reclaiming Stolen Intimacy is a unique experiential resource designed to walk you through the experiences, feelings, and struggles that are common to homes invaded by pornography and other sex addictions. This experience will help group members to be real about their hurts and fears. It will also guide you on a healing journey that requires you to deeply trust God as He leads you down unfamiliar paths. Best of all, you'll join with others on the journey to find that healing occurs best within a caring community.

EDITOR'S NOTE: We realize that not every woman who works through this study is married. However, for the sake of simplicity and clarity, the word "husband" is used throughout the study.

THIS CAN'T BE HAPPENING

GETTING STARTED - 15 MINUTES

LEADER: Read the introductory material in the front of this book and the leader's material at the end of the book. The "Getting Started" exercises are designed to help put women at ease and get them talking. Encourage group members to get acquainted with one another. Keep the tone of the conversation light, and be sure everyone has an opportunity to join in the discussion.

SURPRISES

Life is full of pleasant surprises—perhaps a birthday party or an unexpected job promotion. Maybe you've been surprised by a kind gesture such as flowers or a nice card. What about waking to find your children have made breakfast and are serving you in bed! These surprises always brighten your day and give memories that last a long time.

LEADER INSTRUCTIONS FOR THE GROUP EXPERIENCE: Give each person a 3x5-inch card or a sheet of paper and a pen. Together read the instructions and questions. After allowing a couple of minutes to write, go around the group and ask each woman (including yourself) to give her name and share her responses to the three questions regarding her favorite surprise moment.

1. Take a couple of minutes now and list at least one nice surprise that you've had in your life on index card or sheet of paper. Then, as you introduce yourself, share a brief description of your favorite surprise moment.

2. Was your surprise truly a surprise, or did you have a feeling it was coming?

3. How did your surprise make you feel? Explain why your surprise moment was so nice.

LEADER: *After each woman tells about her surprise, encourage group members by sharing the following information. Then open your Bible and read aloud Psalm 34:17-19.*

Most surprises are exciting and fun. They can take your breath away and make you feel special. But some surprises (like having your life interrupted by the revelation of a sexual addiction), not so much. Those also take your breath away, but in a terrible way. And they leave you feeling weak and wounded. Realize that the Lord is near you during this time. His Word is a gift to you, and His love and compassion are there for you.

17 The righteous cry out, and the LORD hears, and delivers them from all their troubles. 18 The LORD is near the brokenhearted; He saves those crushed in spirit. 19 Many adversities come to the one who is righteous, but the LORD delivers him (her) from them all.

PSALM 34:17-19, HCSB

OPENING PRAYER

Father, we love You and we commit this time to You. You love us and hear us when we cry. God, our hearts are broken and we need to feel Your love. Help us to draw closer to You as we open our hearts to hear from You. Heal our hurts, our fears, our anger, and our insecurities. Lord, we know that You love our husbands, and right now we don't know how to feel about this sin in their lives. Please give us a glimpse of Your love for our husbands. Give us Your supernatural love for them to help us love through the pain. Thank You for the bond of support and security within this group of women. We pray this in the mighty name of Jesus. Amen.

OBJECTIVES FOR THIS SESSION

- Discuss the astonishing statistics of pornography.

- Discover that you are not alone as you experience the hurt inflicted by pornography.

- Recognize that there's a villain in the story, and examine how our enemy, Satan, seeks to destroy Christian marriage.

- Embrace this group of women and establish relationships with those joining you on this journey. (You may not precisely identify with everyone in this room, but you can commit to walk through this study with each other, seeking God's restoration and healing for each woman and her marriage.)

DISCOVERING THE TRUTH – 35 MINUTES

LEADER: *"Discovering the Truth" lays the groundwork to understand key issues in pornography, sexual addiction, and healing. Ask for volunteers to read any Bible passages aloud. Be sure to leave time for the "Embracing the Truth" and "Connecting" segments that follow.*

WHEN THE TRUTH BREAKS YOUR HEART

Most of us sitting in this group find ourselves in a fog of disbelief. Now that the bomb has gone off in our homes and hearts, we're left with a hurtful and embarrassing mess. We may be swallowing hard the words: *"That will never happen to me."* We're brokenhearted.

"The woman who experiences a broken heart, in many ways, is a 'victim' in the wake of another person's actions, whether intentional or unintentional. The broken heart she experiences may be the result of abandonment, rejection, oppression, abuse, or even death. Regardless of the cause, the typical feeling is one of being devastated or feeling as if life has been shattered. Three other emotions are usually quick to arise: fear, loneliness, and despair. In many ways a broken heart is a 'broken spirit,' in which you may lose the will to live, to love, or to trust."[1]

1. In what ways can you relate to this description of being brokenhearted? How so?

When you feel overwhelmed, breathe this promise: *"The LORD is near the brokenhearted."*[2]

HAGAR: MISTREATED AND FEELING DEFEATED

The angel also said, "You are now pregnant and will give birth to a son. You are to name him Ishmael (which means 'God hears'), for the LORD has heard about your misery."

GENESIS 16:11, NLT

In a very difficult time in her life Hagar began to see the God who cares. Before her son was born, God instructed Hagar to name her son Ishmael—"God hears." As so often happens with us, Hagar seems to have forgotten God's dramatic rescue years before and the ongoing reminder that God sees and God hears—*Ishmael.*

¹⁴ Abraham got up early the next morning, prepared food and a container of water, and strapped them on Hagar's shoulders. Then he sent her away with their son, and she wandered aimlessly in the wilderness of Beersheba. ¹⁵ When the water was gone, she put the boy in the shade of a bush ¹⁶ Then she went and sat down by herself about a hundred yards away. "I don't want to watch the boy die," she said, as she burst into tears. ¹⁷ But God heard the boy crying, and the angel of God called to Hagar from heaven, "Hagar, what's wrong? Do not be afraid! God has heard the boy crying as he lies there. ¹⁸ Go to him and comfort him, for I will make a great nation from his descendants." ¹⁹ Then God opened Hagar's eyes, and she saw a well full of water. She quickly filled her water container and gave the boy a drink. ²⁰ And God was with the boy as he grew up in the wilderness. He became a skillful archer, ²¹ and he settled in the wilderness of Paran. His mother arranged for him to marry a woman from the land of Egypt.

GENESIS 21:14-21, NLT

2. Do you wonder if God sees the pain you're going through right now? How do you think He feels about you and your situation?

3. Notice in verse 17 that in the angel's questioning, he's forcing Hagar to feel her own weakness, lack of wisdom, and powerlessness. In doing this, he opens her mind to the fact that God alone is in control. In what ways is it comforting for you to know that God is in control? What can make this difficult for you to accept sometimes?

Earlier in Genesis 16, Hagar had run away because of Sarah's mistreatment toward her. Pregnant, alone, and afraid, the angel of the Lord found Hagar beside a spring of water in the wilderness. At that time, Hagar addressed God as *El Roi*, or "the God who sees me." Notably, this is the only occurrence of *El Roi* in the Bible. As you pray this week, call out to God using this name: *"El Roi,"* for He is the God who sees you. Ask Him to open your eyes to His work in the midst of your struggles.

¹³ Thereafter, Hagar used another name to refer to the LORD, who had spoken to her. She said, "You are the God who sees me." She also said, "Have I truly seen the One who sees me?" ¹⁴ So that well was named Beer-lahai-roi (which means "well of the Living One who sees me").

GENESIS 16:13-14, NLT

LIFE PRINCIPLE

Even when you are unable to cry out to God, He's still the God who hears. He will come to your rescue, but He also wants to open your eyes to the Larger Story and to the resources He's provided so you can join Him in His redemptive mission.

A New Set of Eyes

We all struggle with the age-old question: "Why is there so much suffering in this life?" Like Hagar, we struggle to make sense of emotional pain and deal with it in our own ways.

4. Discuss ways that people tend to deal with hurt, rejection, injustice, and other suffering in their lives. Then read Romans 8:25-28.

[25] But if we hope for what we do not see, with perseverance we wait eagerly for it. [26] In the same way the Spirit also helps our weakness; for we do not know how to pray as we should, but the Spirit Himself intercedes for us with groanings too deep for words; [27] and He who searches the hearts knows what the mind of the Spirit is, because He intercedes for the saints according to the will of God. [28] And we know that God causes all things to work together for good to those who love God, to those who are called according to His purpose.

ROMANS 8:25-28, NASB

5. According to Romans 8:25-28, where is God when we're suffering and struggling? How does it change your perspective or feelings to know that it's not all up to you to make things right and to take care of yourself?

6. In what ways does the truth of Romans 8:28 open our eyes to the larger picture of what God is doing? What attitudes would you expect to see in a person who fully lived the promise of verse 28?

LIFE PRINCIPLE

God made each of us for a purpose, and He allows our suffering only when it's consistent with His work of redemption in our lives. Every moment, every experience, has eternal significance. When you view your experiences—good or bad—as part of God's greater eternal purpose, you'll find peace even in the midst of turmoil.

LEADER: *Discuss as many discovery questions as time permits. Encourage participation by inviting different individuals to respond. Read the questions and explanations for the group. It will help to highlight in advance the questions you want to be certain to include.*

FACING THE UGLY FACTS (THE CULTURAL ASSAULT)

Go to the mall. Open the newspaper. Turn on your TV or computer. Cleavage and rude sexual innuendo is the norm. It's no secret that we live in an extremely perverse time—one where the primary marketing message is "sex sells." Even the most disciplined person can't escape seeing or hearing something sexual from time to time. *Embarrassment* and *shame* are two words that describe the feelings of many wives searching for answers after the reality of sexual sin hits home. We are consumed with the question: *"What will other people think?"*

7. Before this meeting, how many other people have you told about your husband's addiction? How are embarrassment and shame affecting you?

"Those who look to Him are radiant with joy; their faces will never be ashamed" (Psalm 34:5, HCSB). You may have heard it said: "Hate the sin, love the sinner." That's a tall order, especially when it's your husband and his sin in the mix. It's hard to feel "radiant" but you *can* be radiant! You are here seeking God, and there's no shame involved in that ... only light!

VITAL STATISTICS

The Internet has made pornography easily accessible. Gone are the days where a man had to drive to the seedy side of town, get out of his car, and walk into a store to purchase pornographic materials. Now, at the click of a mouse, porn is laid before his eyes.

• Pornography is just as common in the Christian community as it is in society at large.

• It's suggested that $10 billion is spent annually on pornography.

- Revenue from pornography is bigger than the combined revenues of all the professional football, baseball, and basketball franchises.

- U.S. porn revenue exceeds the combined revenues of the four major TV networks.

- There are 68 million daily porn search requests on the Internet. Annually there are 72 million visitors to porn sites worldwide. Daily pornographic e-mails reach 2.5 billion.

- Nine out of 10 children ages 8-16 have been exposed to pornography on the Internet.[3]

8. As you let the statistics really sink in, how much do they surprise you? Write down and discuss a few of the feelings you have after reviewing these statistics. (Feel free to vent.)

9. We all ask, "How could I *not* have noticed my husband's temptation by this sin?" Were there even subtle glimpses into his struggle? What are your thoughts in hindsight?

One question continues to resurface: *"Why did he do this?"* Please understand that your husband is wired completely different than you. He is visual, but keep in mind that God is not surprised because His perfect design included making your husband this way. Recognize that temptation of the eyes for him is very real—very naturally driven.

EMBRACING THE TRUTH – 20 MINUTES

A SPIRITUAL ASSAULT

Be sober! Be on the alert! Your adversary the Devil is prowling around like a roaring lion, looking for anyone he can devour.

1 PETER 5:8, HCSB

1. Our enemy Satan has found an area of weakness in our husbands. Do you recognize that he wants to destroy your marriage and your husband's life? How does this change your perception of your husband's sin and about who needs to be the target of your anger?

[21] *Submit to one another out of reverence for Christ.* [22] *Wives, submit to your husbands, as to the Lord.* [23] *For the husband is the head of the wife as also Christ is head of the church.*

EPHESIANS 5:21-23, NIV

2. What's the significance of the command in verse 25? Give examples of Christ's love for us. How does sexual sin in a marriage damage this model of a sacrificial, covenant marriage?

AN ENEMY ATTACK/A PROMISE BROKEN

"Every step toward intimacy must be balanced by faithfulness and tenderness. Love develops as you simultaneously move in faithfulness toward an exclusive commitment and in tenderness toward a unique intimacy."[4]

3. In your heart are you wrestling with thoughts such as: *If he loves me, why did he do this?* or *I trusted him; how could he hurt me like this?* It's important to be honest with yourself as you share some of your burning questions with the group.

A powerful and destructive enemy has invaded your marriage. That promise of faithfulness at the wedding altar has been broken by sexual sin. The road to healing for your husband will take time, and he will need support from many people—you included.

It can be very tough to see any good coming from such a hurtful situation. During times of hopelessness, we must cling to Genesis 50:20: *"You planned evil against me; God planned it for good."* Ruth Graham (daughter of Billy and Ruth Graham) described a moment of hurt in her life after her husband's confession of an affair to the pastor and elders of their church. When everyone rushed around him and embraced *him* in love, it felt to her like a truck had run over her. And then it backed up and ran over her again. Everyone who witnessed the accident ran to check on the truck driver, while she lay in the street battered and bleeding. **Wow. Paints a very clear picture, doesn't it?**

4. If you had to describe a large object that just ran over you, what would it be? If your husband is seeking forgiveness and counseling, what are your feelings about the attention he's receiving? Write down specific words that describe how you feel.

Even if your husband has humbly confessed and is willing to seek help, you may still find resentment or anger in your heart. You also may resent the attention he's receiving.

5. Would it be possible, even in this early discussion, to ask God to give you a heart of compassion toward your husband? What are some barriers for you right now?

HOPE: A REAL POSSIBILITY

Every feeling you're experiencing is valid. Don't discount those feelings ... because they're real. But please add something new today to what you're feeling—*HOPE*. Our hope is not in our husbands winning this battle, but in our God who fights our battles for us.

For the LORD your God is the one who goes with you to fight for you against your enemies to give you victory.

DEUTERONOMY 20:4, NIV

LEADER INSTRUCTIONS FOR THE GROUP EXPERIENCE: Have a CD player ready to play the song, "Untitled Hymn: Come to Jesus" by Chris Rice. Locate the album Run the Earth, Watch the Skies *or download the song. Consider playing only the melody while reading aloud the Luke 8:43-48 passage and then playing the full song with verses immediately after that.*

---

[43] A woman suffering from bleeding for 12 years, who had spent all she had on doctors yet could not be healed by any, [44] approached from behind and touched the tassel of His robe. Instantly her bleeding stopped. [45] "Who touched Me?" Jesus asked. When they all denied it, Peter said, "Master, the crowds are hemming You in and pressing against You." [46] "Somebody did touch Me," said Jesus. "I know that power has gone out from Me." [47] When the woman saw that she was discovered, she came trembling and fell down before Him. In the presence of all the people, she declared the reason she had touched Him and how she was instantly cured. [48] "Daughter," He said to her, "your faith has made you well. Go in peace."

LUKE 8:43-48, HCSB

6. If you had been the woman in Luke 8:43-48 with the bleeding issue and had spent all the money you had on doctors, how would you have felt? Why?

7. What one thing did she have left when she pushed though the crowd and touched Jesus' robe? What difference did it make?

IMPORTANT: Holding onto anger and bitterness can definitely make us ill physically and spiritually. It can shut us down. Today, push through the throng of perversion and relational devastation in society and grab hold of Jesus. He *will* heal your heart.

RECLAIMING YOUR LIFE TOGETHER

On the journey to reclaiming stolen intimacy we will see this map unfold. The map will help us understand where we are in the process while keeping the destination clearly in focus. The journey begins when we make the decision to choose healing.

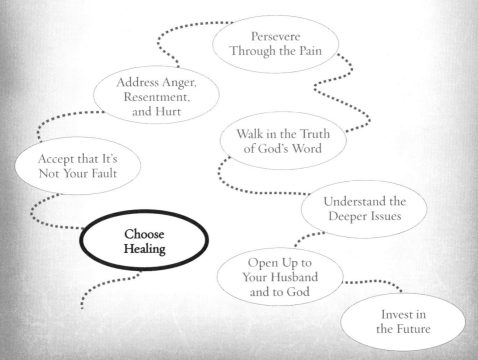

CONNECTING – 20 Minutes

LEADER: *"Connecting" is a time to help group members connect with one another, with God, and with their own hearts. Read aloud the "Letter from a Wife" to get the sharing going. Also be prepared to share your story to set the tone of openness and trust. Those more reluctant to open up will benefit from hearing your story and the stories of others. Invite everyone to join into the discussions.*

LETTER FROM A WIFE

"We are dealing with the sin of my husband viewing porn. I found out shortly after we were married that he had been doing this since he was 12 years old. We talked about it and dealt with it the best we knew how at the time. We even met with our pastor and started to learn how to build hedges that would help protect him from this temptation. We prayed about it and dealt with it for a while and then it got lost in the shuffle. Occasionally I would ask how he was doing, and he would sometimes confess that he had backslidden (gotta love the Christian lingo). I would forgive and move on.

"Then a few weeks ago I looked at the history on our computer and found things I did NOT want to find! It hit me hard this time. I was so hurt. We had just had an awesome weekend with each other which involved 'husband-wife time' so I thought things were going great. Not that having a long weekend with intimacy makes your marriage great, but I felt like it just still wasn't enough for him. I confronted him. I actually punched him in the shoulder because I couldn't get the words out at first. Then I broke down and told him this really hurt me this time. I mean, it hurt before, but for some reason it was different this time.

"For the first time, he was truly broken about his sin. We both cried. He has been talking with our small-group leader from church and praying with him. I have been praying for him (which is something I rarely did before). I feel like we are on the right path, but at the same time I just feel kind of lost. God has shown me that I need to cling to Christ first and foremost in every situation in my life."

1. What are you feeling right now after hearing this woman's story and thinking about your own? **Take a few moments now to write a personal letter to God in the space provided on the next page.** Include how your husband's sin has impacted your life. Express the emotions you're feeling. You may not fully believe it yet, but still, end your letter on an upbeat note of hope for what God is going to do.

_____

_____

_____

_____

_____

_____

_____

_____

2. If you feel comfortable, read some or all of your letter aloud to the group. Avoid using this opportunity as a time to bash your husband. Just read what you've written and move on. This group is a safe place for you to vent your frustrations as well as share together in the victories you will see throughout this study.

The opportunity to hear from other women in your group will help you connect and better know how to pray for one another. NOTE: There will be various stages and degrees of hurt and difficulty represented by the women in this group. Please be sensitive to each other during this study.

MY PRAYER NEEDS (List your needs.)

MY GROUP'S PRAYER NEEDS (Note: keep this list confidential. See Group Covenant, page 21.)

TAKING IT HOME

QUESTIONS TO TAKE TO MY HEART

Please take time this week to journal your thoughts from this first meeting. If you were unable to complete your letter to God, do that now. Perhaps you would like to write another letter if you find that your feelings are changing in any way.

Answer the questions honestly. Grapple with what drives your thinking and behavior. Our behaviors are the best indicators of what we really believe in our heart of hearts rather than our surface beliefs. Seek to understand what you believe in your innermost being (Psalm 51:6, NASB) about God, yourself, and the world in which you live.

> ✳ **Have my emotions from dealing with my situation negatively impacted the way I react to my children? My friends?**

✳ Do I really want to forgive my husband? What's preventing me from asking God to help me begin to let go of my anger and bitterness?

✳ What impact, if any, would my husband feel if he knew that I truly wanted to forgive him and had already begun going to God on his behalf?

TIME FOR YOU

Mostly likely you're expending a lot of time and energy dealing with this situation. However it is important that you take care of yourself too. Most of us struggle with the fact that there aren't enough hours in the day, and the demands of being wives, mothers, employees, and so forth leave us overworked, underpaid, and drained. Exercise! Go for a 20-minute walk—especially in a moment when you're feeling angry. Just think—a fringe benefit is you could potentially burn off massive amounts of calories! Join a gym or your local YMCA. Call a friend and go to a spa. If budget is a concern, call a local cosmetology school and ask if they do manicures and pedicures. Taking this time for you will make you feel loved and cared for. Don't neglect yourself during this process.

In I Corinthians 6:20 (NLT) we are told: *"God bought you with a high price. So you must honor God with your body."* Taking care of your body is honoring to God.

NOTES:

1. The Woman's Study Bible (Nashville: Thomas Nelson Publishers, 1995).

2. Psalm 34:18

3. National Coalition for the Protection of Children & Families. [cited 13 May 2008]. Available from the Internet: *www.nationalcoalition.org/statisticspornography.asp*

4. Walter Trobisch, *I Married You* (Boliver, MO: Quiet Waters Publication, 1971).

How I'm Feeling Really

Group Covenant

As you begin this study, it is important that your group covenant together, agreeing to live out important group values. Once these values are agreed upon, your group will be on its way to experiencing true redemptive community. It's very important that your group discuss these values—preferably as you begin this study.

* PRIORITY: While we are in this group, we will give the group meetings priority. All the sessions are integrated, with each session building on the sessions that precede them. Committed attendance is vital to overcoming your addictions.

  NOTE: Due to the focus of this group on taking the journey to freedom, group sessions will require a full 90 minutes to complete, so plan accordingly.

* PARTICIPATION AND FAIRNESS: Because we are here to receive help, we commit to participation and interaction in the group. No one dominates. We will be fair to others and concentrate on telling our own stories briefly.

* HOMEWORK: The homework experiences are an integral and vital part of the recovery process. The assignments between each session might include: (1) A Question to Take to My Heart; (2) A Question to Take to God; and (3) Journal activities that must be completed to continue on with your healing journey.

* RESPECT AND OWNERSHIP: Everyone is given the right to his or her own opinions, and all questions are encouraged and respected. We will not judge or condemn as others share their stories. We are each responsible for our own recovery and will not "own" someone else's. Offensive language is not permitted.

* CONFIDENTIALITY: Anything said in our meetings is never repeated outside the meeting without permission of all of group members. This is vital in creating the environment of trust and openness required to facilitate the healing and freedom. Names of attendees will not be shared with others. NOTE: Check state and federal laws governing pastoral and counselor reporting requirements for any known criminal activities.

* LIFE CHANGE: We will regularly assess our progress and will complete the "Taking it Home" activities to reinforce what we are learning and better integrate those lessons into our personal journeys.

* CARE AND SUPPORT: Permission is given to call upon each other at any time, especially in times of crisis. The group will provide care for every member.

* ACCOUNTABILITY AND INTEGRITY: We agree to let the members of our group hold us accountable to commitments we make in whatever loving ways we decide upon. Unsolicited advice giving is not permitted. We will seek out and build a close relationship with accountability partners for mutual growth and responsibility.

* EXPECTATIONS OF FACILITATORS: This meeting is not professional therapy. We are not licensed therapists. Group facilitators are volunteers whose only desire is to encourage people in finding freedom and hope.

I agree to all of the above _____ Date _____

Is This My Fault?

Getting Started - 15 minutes

LEADER: *The "Getting Started" exercise will help put group members at ease and continue to help them connect with one another. To be sure everyone gets a turn, encourage the women to be brief.*

LEADER INSTRUCTIONS FOR THE GROUP EXPERIENCE: (1) Provide magazines on a variety of topics (home improvement, gardening, fashion, and others). (2) Give group members five minutes to browse the magazines and note pictures and articles focused on improvement. (3) Ask a couple of women to share their observations. (4) Ask each woman to write her best physical attribute and her best spiritual attribute on a 3x5-inch card. Then, read the following notes and discuss the questions that follow. Be sensitive to those who are not yet ready to open up.

On any given photo shoot or movie set, there's a team of make-up artists, lighting experts, and image coaches. And after the photo shoot, another team wades into the world of Photoshop® to digitally enhance the images. If we asked the question: "Are you satisfied with your body?" most of us would answer: "No!" How can we measure up to those "perfect" images? Well, let's say it together: "**We can't!**"

TV makeover programs cover every topic. They tell us what we have isn't sufficient and make us want more—the perfect lawn, kitchen, hair, or body. And just when we get our hands on the new "in thing," society changes what's "in." It's a cycle of discontentment.

1. **Let's examine our own personal wish lists.** If you could be on one of those makeover shows, what would be your first choice to change about yourself or your home?

2. How do the images we see daily influence or shape our choices? our self-images?

3. Write your best physical and spiritual attributes on a 3x5-inch card. Share what you wrote with the group, and then place your card in a visible spot in your home. Thank God for His gift of these attributes in your life.

OPENING PRAYER

O God, meet us here. We're wounded and confused. We need to feel Your guidance through this time. Lord, we're insecure and need to be filled with the security that only You can bring into our lives. Let us feel Your presence. We ask You to replace the doubt and fear we're carrying with Your peace. Protect us from the Enemy because we know his questions make us doubt and blame. We ask You to shut him down. In the very strong name of Jesus, Amen.

OBJECTIVES FOR THIS SESSION

• Examine the negative impact the world and the Enemy have on our self-esteem.

• Discuss the effect and drawing power of pornography on a man.

• Understand and accept that your husband's area of weakness is not your fault.

• Embrace Scriptures that build your self-esteem in Christ.

DISCOVERING THE TRUTH – 35 MINUTES

LEADER: *Briefly review your progress on the "Reclaiming your Life Together" diagram, and then summarize the material in the section "It's Not Your Fault." As you discuss the questions, make sure to leave time for "Embracing the Truth" and the "Connecting" group experience that follow.*

RECLAIMING YOUR LIFE TOGETHER

On the journey to reclaiming stolen intimacy we will see the map unfold. The map will help us understand where we are in the process while keeping the destination clearly in mind.

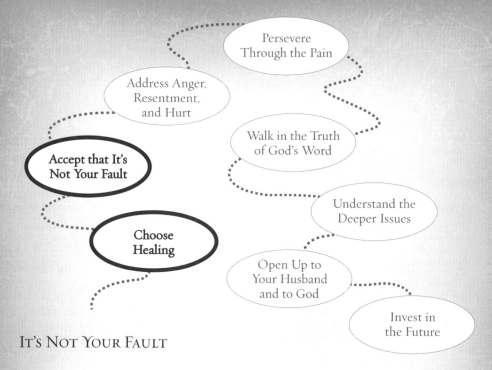

Persevere
Through the Pain

Address Anger,
Resentment,
and Hurt

Walk in the Truth
of God's Word

**Accept that It's
Not Your Fault**

Understand the
Deeper Issues

**Choose
Healing**

Open Up to
Your Husband
and to God

Invest in
the Future

It's Not Your Fault

After coming to terms with the realization that pornography has invaded our lives, one question rings louder than almost any other: *"Is this my fault?"* Sex-related addictions invade the most vulnerable and private aspect of our lives, intimacy, and security.

Porn wreaks havoc on our already battered self-esteems. Take a look at the impact experts warn that viewing pornography has on people:

"Pornography assaults the senses and sensibilities of the Christian. Scripture admonishes us to live holy and moral lives ... and to respect every God-created individual. ... It's most devastating aspect is the false presentation of women and children as sexual objects who supposedly enjoy brutality and violence. Pornography encourages images that are antithetical to the biblical concept of sexuality and features a degrading and unrealistic portrayal of sexual intimacy. It condones anti-social, destructive behavior, and its use has a subtle, drugging effect on morality. Pornography becomes a moral problem in that it subordinates and exploits God's plan for sexuality and encourages sadistic and violent practices. To assume that porn has no influence on behavior is naïve at best and irresponsible at worst."[1]

1. Has the revelation of your husband's struggle made you feel that he finds you unattractive? Do you fear that his engaging with porn has made it impossible for you to please him? Share your fears with the group (as you're comfortable).

2. To what level do you imagine scenarios of your husband giving in to the temptation to lust throughout the day? doubting where he is or what he's looking at on the computer? Write some of your fears and doubts below and share one with the group.

Is It Me?

LEADER INSTRUCTIONS FOR THE GROUP EXPERIENCE: *Provide a CD player and the* CD Somebody's Daughter *available from Serendipity. Ask group members to close their eyes and listen to the song "Is It Me?" Give a few moments for personal reflection at the end of the song and then discuss the questions that follow.*

3. With what feelings in the song "Is It Me?" can you identify? Write them down now and discuss one within your group.

4. The song clearly reflects a struggle going on between her mind and her heart. Consider these lyrics: "*I hate you! I hate that I need you! Only God can save us!*" What inner struggles does the song highlight? Name a couple of your inner struggles.

LIFE PRINCIPLE
While all relational issues are two-sided, it's important to recognize that your husband's failures and sins related to sexual addiction and pornography are NOT your fault. The Enemy lured him in and he chose to take the bait.

LEADER: *Ask three group members to read one each of the stories from hurting wives. Discuss the questions following each story.*

Porn is a deceiver and a mockery of the sexuality God created between a husband and wife: sex designed to be mutually enjoyable and exclusively intimate. It also damages the living illustration of God's personal, exclusive, intimate care for each one of His people.

Letter from a Hurting Wife

"Throughout our marriage, he has made little remarks about me. On our honeymoon he told me to take an outfit off because a Christian wife isn't supposed to wear things like that. So for 15 years I didn't. Within five days of his pornography confession, I gave away over half my clothes and decided to dress more contemporary. On our vacation I noticed my husband staring at a woman in a swimsuit. When I asked him about this, he told me that because I didn't have large breasts and my hips were bigger after the birth of our children, he wasn't sexually attracted to me anymore. We separated for some time, and after much counseling we have reconciled but still have many miles to go. He wants to be with me intimately but says he placed me so far away from the sin he viewed that he is still confused about how to view me as his wife."

Letter from another Hurting Wife

"Doubt starts creeping in and making me question whether there was something I could've or should've been doing differently to try and prevent this situation. I know that's not right. I know this isn't my fault, and he was still the one who had to make the choice to go to those Web sites. I really do feel like I was being incredibly sensitive to his needs and that there is nothing that I could've done differently … but doubt is a powerful thing. But where it really hits below the belt is the fact that I have been struggling with my weight my entire life, and knowing that he was looking at all those gorgeous women doesn't exactly work wonders for my self-esteem. It hurts! I've managed to lose 40 pounds in the last year, and he still felt the need to turn to porn. That really hurts."

5. Do you feel the kinds of doubts the two women expressed in their letters? If so, which doubts resonate with your story?

6. How has your husband's involvement with pornography affected your sexual relationship? (Are you repulsed or insecure? Do you withhold yourself from him because of this?) How do you feel about your ability to meet his sexual needs?

Most of us don't have pornography in our homes, but many of us have magazine subscriptions that we enjoy. Sometimes these magazines, as well as movies, music, and catalogs, can add fuel to the fire with their sexually suggestive material.

RENEE'S PERSONAL STORY

"Talk about pouring fuel on the fire ... I ordered a swimsuit from my sister's Victoria's Secret® catalog, so I began receiving their weekly catalogs. One day Clay approached me and said that seeing those catalogs laying around the house was a real temptation for him. This was the first time I had ever thought about it. As I looked at the catalog through his eyes, I saw where this could be a real struggle for any male. The poses and the eyes were seductive and sexual in nature. I called and canceled my catalog subscription. I still shop there for something nice on occasion, but I don't want the catalogs piling up and causing my husband to stumble. This experience made me examine all of the magazines I had coming into the house."

Death and Destruction are never satisfied, and neither are the eyes of man. Hell has a voracious appetite, and lust just never quits.   PROVERBS 27:20, NIV

7. Our husbands are visually stimulated. Discuss any kind of suggestive material you may have in your homes. What tradeoffs would you have to make to dispose of it? In what ways can you be more careful with what you bring into your home? What would it take to install filtering/accountability software on your computers?

SEDUCTION'S TRAP

It's natural to view our husbands as our enemies when we feel betrayed. In session 1, though, we identified the true Villain as Satan, the ravenous lion (1 Peter 5:8). God warned Cain in Genesis 4:7—"Sin is crouching at the door. Its desire is for you, but you must master it" (HCSB). It might help you to move forward on your healing journey to consider the Enemy's cunning and vicious attacks on your husband and on your marriage.

[5:3] Though the lips of the forbidden woman drip honey and her words are smoother than oil, [4] in the end she's as bitter as wormwood and as sharp as a double-edged sword. [6:25] Don't lust in your heart for her beauty or let her captivate you with her eyelashes. [26] For a prostitute's fee is only a loaf of bread, but an adulteress goes after your very life. [7:21] She seduces him with her persistent pleading; she lures with her flattering talk. [22] He follows her impulsively like an ox going to the slaughter, like a deer bounding toward a trap. [23:27] For a prostitute is a deep pit, and a forbidden woman is a narrow well; [28] indeed, she sets an ambush like a robber and increases those among men who are unfaithful.

PROVERBS 5:3-4; 6:25-26; 7:21-22; 23:27-28, HCSB

8. How does the seductress in Proverbs lure men with her wiles and cunning? Why is sexual temptation such a vicious trap?

9. What factors do you think add to a man's vulnerability to take give in to temptation?

Pray silently for your husband now. Pray that he recognizes the draw of sexual sin in his life and the danger of its trap. Pray too that he fully understands the hurt his secret seductress has caused you. Ask God to open his eyes and his heart to your pain.

EMBRACING THE TRUTH – 20 MINUTES

LEADER: *"Embracing the Truth" is the section in which group members focus on integrating the truth they're learning into their hearts and lives. Be aware that the level of hurt and response to hurt will be different for each woman. Therefore the rate of life application will vary accordingly.*

Our self-esteem has taken a beating because of our husbands' struggles. It's normal and typical to ask ourselves: *How can he really love me? Why did he go elsewhere for sexual satisfaction? Is there something wrong with me? Where do I turn to for a true guide to a healthy view of myself?*

1. What are some of the places we typically turn for guidance in repairing our self-esteem or for a scale to measure our value?

You won't find the answer to a healthy self-esteem from women's magazines nor from any talk shows. You must daily bathe in the truth of God's words to us. It's important that you have an accurate and healthy self-image. God wants to cover you in the soothing comfort that your image emerges from His image.

²⁶ *Then God said, "Let us make people in our image, to be like Ourselves." ... ²⁷ So God created human beings in his own image. In the image of God he created them; male and female he created them.*

GENESIS 1:26-27, NLT

³ *When I observe Your heavens, the work of Your fingers, the moon and the stars, which You set in place, ⁴ what is man that You remember him, the son of man that You look after him? ⁵ You made him little less than God and crowned him with glory and honor.*

PSALM 8:3-5, HCSB

2. According to Genesis 1 and Psalm 8, what's the most fundamental thing about who we are—our identity? How could this truth transform the way we see ourselves?

LIFE PRINCIPLE

Poor self-esteem is a heavy weight that keeps you under condemnation and causes you to be less than what God intends. As one of God's image-bearers, you need to combat such feelings of inferiority. God wants you to live as the royal beauty He created you to be, clothed in His glory and majesty.

LEADER: *As time permits, ask group members to locate some verses listed in the following bullets and read them aloud. Otherwise, encourage the ladies to review these powerful verses at home.*

Prerequisites for a Healthy Self-Esteem

- Recognize your ongoing need for a Savior (*Isaiah 53:6; Job 19:25*)

- Understand that your life is hidden with Christ in God (*Colossians 3:3-4*)

- Embrace the truth that you no longer live under condemnation; Christ has set you free (*Romans 8:1; Galatians 5:1*)

- Trust that God's heart is good and that He cares deeply for you (*Romans 8:28; 1 Peter 5:16-17*)

- Press forward in God's plan for your life (*Philippians 3:13-14*)

- Accept a realistic view of yourself (*Romans 12:3; Psalm 8:3-5; 103:13-14*)

- Avoid comparisons to others (*2 Corinthians 10:12*)

Proper self-esteem involves recognizing and confronting yourself in your humanity, including the tendency to sin—to go our own way. It also embraces Jesus' work on the cross and His grace that covers a multitude of sins. Comprehending God's infinite care for you and understanding your true identity in Christ realigns your view of yourself.

Characteristics of Healthy Self-Esteem

- Resting in God's ownership of you and your life (*1 Corinthians 3:16; Isaiah 41:10*)

- Submitting to being a special "workmanship" of God (*Ephesians 2:10; Psalm 139:14*)

- Appreciating the differences of others (*1 Corinthians 12:1-31*)

- Willing to take risks and steps of faith (*Esther 4:13-16*)

- Forging redemptive relationships with others (*Ruth 1:16-17; James 5:16*)

- Living with the knowledge that your life is hidden with Christ in God (*Colossians 3:3-4*)

3. Look again at the lists of prerequisites and characteristics of healthy self-esteem. Which one or two areas create the greatest challenge for you? Give an example.

"God does not evaluate human worth as we do. He looks to the heart within, while we tend to only look at the outer frame. ... The heart of a healthy self-esteem is recognizing that 'self' must be seen as created for God's glory. We might more accurately say that within every believer there must be 'God-esteem,' which accepts whatever lot in life is ours. ... God does not make mistakes, and He is never finished working in us as He continues to refine and edify, helping each woman reach her maximum potential."[2]

² Praise the LORD, O my soul, and forget not all his benefits—³ who forgives all your sins and heals all your diseases, ⁴ who redeems your life from the pit and crowns you with love and compassion, ⁵ who satisfies your desires with good things so that your youth is renewed like the eagle's. ... ¹³ As a father has compassion on his children, so the LORD has compassion on those who fear him; ¹⁴ for he knows how we are formed, he remembers that we are dust.

PSALM 103:2-5,13-14

¹³ You made all the delicate, inner parts of my body and knit me together in my mother's womb. ¹⁴ Thank you for making me so wonderfully complex! Your workmanship is marvelous—how well I know it. ¹⁵ You watched me as I was being formed in utter seclusion, as I was woven together in the dark of the womb. ¹⁶ You saw me before I was born. Every day of my life was recorded in your book. Every moment was laid out before a single day had passed.

PSALM 139:13-16, NLT

4. According to Psalm 103, how does God view and relate to us? What level of performance or perfection does He expect or require from us?

5. Note in Psalm 139:13-16 the care and attention that God gave to your creation. How does reading this passage and Psalm 103 make you feel?

CONNECTING – 20 MINUTES

GOD KNOWS AND CARES DEEPLY ABOUT HOW YOU'RE COPING

> **LEADER:** *Use "Connecting" as a time to help group members connect with one another, with God, and with their own hearts. Be prepared to share your story to establish the tone of openness and trust. Those who are more reluctant to open up will benefit greatly from hearing your story and the stories of others. Invite everyone to join into the discussions.*

1. Divide into three subgroups when instructed by your leader and review the psalm you're assigned. Take 10 minutes or less to capture three lists on the paper provided:

   1) **What issues** past or current is the psalmist facing?
   2) **What has God done** for the psalmist?
   3) **Why does the psalmist trust** his future to God?

GROUP 1:

⁸ You [God] keep track of all my sorrows. You have collected all my tears in your bottle. You have recorded each one in your book. ⁹ My enemies will retreat when I call to you for help. This I know: God is on my side! ¹⁰ I praise God for what he has promised; yes, I praise the LORD for what he has promised. ¹¹ I trust in God, so why should I be afraid? What can mere mortals do to me? ¹² I will fulfill my vows to you, O God, and will offer a sacrifice of thanks for your help. ¹³ For you have rescued me from death; you have kept my feet from slipping. So now I can walk in your presence, O God, in your life-giving light.

PSALM 56:8-13, NLT

GROUP 2:

⁷ I will bless the LORD who guides me; even at night my heart instructs me. ⁸ I know the LORD is always with me. I will not be shaken, for he is right beside me. ⁹ No wonder my heart is glad, and I rejoice. My body rests in safety. ¹⁰ For you will not leave my soul among the dead or allow your holy one to rot in the grave. ¹¹ You will show me the way of life, granting me the joy of your presence and the pleasures of living with you forever.

PSALM 16:7-11, NLT

Guard me as the apple of Your eye; hide me in the shadow of Your wings.   PSALM 17:8, HCSB

GROUP 3:

² Be merciful to me, LORD, for I am faint; O LORD, heal me, for my bones are in agony. ³ My soul is in anguish. How long, O LORD, how long? ⁴ Turn, O LORD, and deliver me; save me because of your unfailing love. ⁵ No one remembers you when he is dead. Who praises you from the grave? ⁶ I am worn out from groaning; all night long I flood my bed with weeping and drench my couch with tears. ⁷ My eyes grow weak with sorrow; they fail because of all my foes. ⁸ Away from me, all you who do evil, for the LORD has heard my weeping. ⁹ The LORD has heard my cry for mercy; the LORD accepts my prayer. ¹⁰ All my enemies will be ashamed and dismayed; they will turn back in sudden disgrace.

PSALM 6:2-10, NIV

2. As you've discussed these psalms, what impression do you get about how God feels about you personally? If you're comfortable sharing, let the group know how you feel about God right now.

3. Have you found yourself being as open and vulnerable with God as the psalmist? How about as confrontational and bold? If you're holding back, why do you think that's happening?

LEADER: *Provide a 3x5-inch card for each woman to take home. Instruct group members to write a word of affirmation this week on a card to the other women. There are instructions in "Taking It Home." Close by sharing and praying for key needs in the group.*

4. God and God alone can give us the focus we need. Meditate for a moment on the chorus of the hymn "Turn Your Eyes upon Jesus":

"Turn your eyes upon Jesus. Look full in His wonderful face. And the things of earth will grow strangely dim in the light of his glory and grace."[3]

MY PRAYER NEEDS

MY GROUP'S PRAYER NEEDS

TAKING IT HOME

QUESTIONS TO TAKE TO GOD

It's time to ask God a couple of questions. Be careful not to rush or manufacture an answer. Don't write down what you think the "right" answer is. Don't turn the Bible into a reference book or spiritual encyclopedia. Just pose a question to God and wait for Him. Anything God speaks will always be consistent with the Scripture. Be sure to write down what you hear from God.

✮ **God, where were You when all this junk was going on in my life?**

✮ **How do You feel about me right now? How about my husband?**

SHARING AFFIRMATION

Sometimes we don't realize what a toll the messages we are bombarded with take on our self-esteem. Everyone needs to feel worth. Spend a few moments affirming the other women in your group. On a 3x5-inch card write a word of affirmation directed toward the women in your group. Put the card in your book and take it with you to the next gathering.

Scripture and Journal Guidance

Read the following passage of Scripture several times this week.

GOD, *investigate my life; get all the facts firsthand. I'm an open book to you; even from a distance, you know what I'm thinking. You know when I leave and when I get back; I'm never out of your sight. You know everything I'm going to say before I start the first sentence. I look behind me and you're there, then up ahead and you're there, too—your reassuring presence, coming and going. This is too much, too wonderful—I can't take it all in!*

Is there anyplace I can go to avoid your Spirit? to be out of your sight? If I climb to the sky, you're there! If I go underground, you're there! If I flew on the morning's wings to the far western horizon, You'd find me in a minute—you're already there waiting! Then I said to myself, "Oh, he even sees me in the dark! At night I'm immersed in the light!" It's a fact: darkness isn't dark to you; night and day, darkness and light, they're all the same to you.

Oh, yes you shaped me first inside, then out; you formed me in my mother's womb. I thank you, High God—you're breathtaking! **Body and soul, I am marvelously made!** *I worship in adoration— what a creation! You know me inside and out, you know every bone in my body, you know exactly how I was made, bit by bit, how I was sculpted from nothing into something. Like an open book, you watched me grow from conception to birth; all the stages of my life were spread out before you, the days of my life all prepared before I'd even lived one day.*

PSALM 139: 1-16, THE MESSAGE

As you reflect on this Scripture passage, journal what God is saying to you. Also include what your heart is saying to you. Are you sensing God's love for you? Why or why not? Does this passage raise a question you'd like to pose to God? If so, ask Him. Journal the question you're asking God. Then watch for His answer over the next weeks and months.

Remember, no circumstance can separate you from the love of the Father. Even before you were created He knew you and had good plans for you. Keep your eyes focused on Him. Take heart and rest under the shadow of His wings!

Time for Me

Remember to take time out for yourself. As we mentioned in session 1, go for a nice walk. As you walk, meditate on passages from Psalm 139. Repeat these over and over in your mind until they penetrate your heart. Remember, God designed you, every part, inside and out. Take care of the gift He has given you. Affirm the positive instead of dwelling on the negative. God will honor this exercise of meditation in your life.

How Close is God to Me?

_____

_____

_____

_____

_____

_____

_____

_____

_____

_____

_____

_____

_____

_____

_____

_____

_____

_____

_____

_____

_____

_____

_____

_____

_____

_____

_____

NOTES:

1. _The Woman's Study Bible_ (Nashville: Thomas Nelson Publishers, 1995).

2. Ibid.

3. Helen H. Lemmel, "Turn Your Eyes upon Jesus" in _The Baptist Hymnal_ (Nashville, TN: Convention Press, 1991), No. 320.

HOW CAN I EVER TRUST HIM AGAIN?

GETTING STARTED - 15 MINUTES

LEADER INSTRUCTIONS FOR THE GROUP EXPERIENCE: Scatter several objects (some messy such as a plastic bowl of dry rice or beans) on the floor around the room to make a small obstacle course. Also bring a blindfold. If time allows, repeat the minefield activity with another pair.

MINEFIELD

Select two women from the group for an activity. Blindfold one. The partner will use only words to guide her blindfolded partner around all the objects and back to her seat.

Questions for the minefield partners:
1. How well were you able to communicate to your partner where you wanted her to go?

2. As you were blindfolded, how easy was it for you to follow your partner's directions? How fully were you able to trust her guidance? Did you feel any hesitancy in trusting during the exercise?

Questions for the whole group:
3. On a scale of 1 to 10, how would you rate your ability to trust your friends? Now rate your ability to trust people in general on the second scale.

I never trust my friends	1	2	3	4	5	6	7	8	9	10	I always trust my friends

I never trust	1	2	3	4	5	6	7	8	9	10	I always trust

Opening Prayer

O, God. Only You can help us here. Only You can meet us in this tremendous area of need. We need You to teach us how to love and trust again. Help us see past the pain and betrayal of this moment and move forward to complete healing and trust in You. Show us Your ways, God, and don't let us lean on our own understanding. Teach us to rely on You. Thanks for walking this road with us. Amen.

Objectives for this Session

- Talk about the emotional roller coaster of hurt and trust.
- Discuss what real forgiveness is and is not. Realize that forgiveness is not optional.
- Examine emotions and truths related to forgiveness and trust.
- Understand our trust should ultimately be in God and not in other people

Discovering the Truth – 40 Minutes

Reclaiming Your Life Together

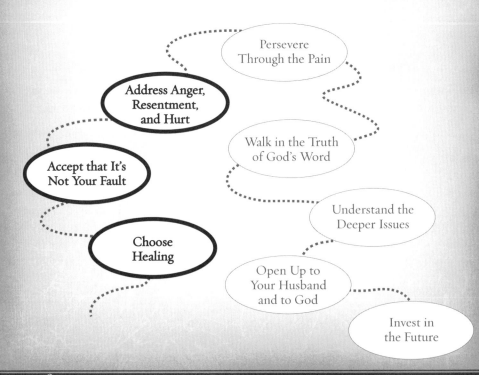

Persevere Through the Pain

Address Anger, Resentment, and Hurt

Accept that It's Not Your Fault

Walk in the Truth of God's Word

Choose Healing

Understand the Deeper Issues

Open Up to Your Husband and to God

Invest in the Future

In our last session, we dealt with the fact that our husbands' sexual sins are not our fault. Even when we accept this truth though, we find ourselves no less angry, resentful, or hurt. The path to healing and redemption of our lives is difficult, but we're on the journey with a group of sisters who are supporting one another.

LEADER: "Discovering the Truth" will focus on understanding forgiveness. Remaining focused on what God says is central to the whole process. Make sure to give women time to reflect on the questions and to share from their hearts. Emphasize the importance of meditating on Scripture and even memorizing several of the Scriptures you'll discuss. Ask a group member to read the letter aloud.

FORGIVENESS IS NEVER WITHOUT SACRIFICE

We now find ourselves on one of the most difficult paths to walk: truly granting forgiveness and rebuilding trust. We would like to forgive, but we've been deeply hurt and betrayed by the actions of our husbands. We must discuss the valid emotions that arise during times like these, including anger, resentment, pain, and other dark emotions.

1. How would you answer the following questions:

- What if my husband doesn't really understand why I feel so hurt?

- What if I can't shake the doubts and fears in my mind?

- What if my husband falls again into this secret, demeaning sin?

LETTER: CONFUSED AND AFRAID

"I find myself after 24 years of marriage unable to trust my husband. He has betrayed me for many years with his secret sin. Even before we had the Internet in our home, he was going to a really bad neighborhood by the airport to purchase pornographic material. After all these years, how can I trust him again? It has become such a part of his life that I can't imagine him being able to quit viewing porn. I want to forget that I ever found out about this and return to 'normal,' but I know that is not reality. I know I should forgive him and try to move on, but I am confused and consumed with fear."

2. If the wife of 24 years chooses to forgive, is she condoning her husband's behavior? Does forgiveness require her to trust her husband right away? Discuss your responses.

3. Forgiveness always requires a sacrifice on the part of the one who forgives. Jesus set the model for sacrifice in dying for our failures and sins. What are some sacrifices a woman might have to make in order to grant forgiveness and let her husband off the hook?

What Forgiveness is Not[1]

Before we discuss the role of forgiveness in healing, let's clarify what forgiveness *is not*.

Forgiveness is NOT forgetting. We frequently hear the phrase "forgive and forget," but forgiveness does not imply amnesia. When the Bible says that God "will remember their sins no more," it doesn't mean that He suddenly has no recollection of an offense. It means that God does not catalog our sins and use the information against us.

Forgiveness is NOT minimizing the hurt. It does not water down the offense by saying, "It's OK, it wasn't that bad," or "I know you didn't mean to hurt me." You've been hurt deeply so don't pretend. Forgiveness calls for truth just like a baseball umpire calls what he sees.

Forgiveness does NOT mean trust is automatic. Forgiveness opens the door to begin the process of reconciling. Rebuilding trust requires time, communication, and accountability. Forgiveness is granted, but trust is earned.

4. Do any of these clarifications of what forgiveness is *not* alter your views about forgiveness? How so?

The Foundation for Forgiveness

[12] *Since God chose you to be the holy people he loves, you must clothe yourselves with tenderhearted mercy, kindness, humility, gentleness, and patience.* [13] *Make allowance for each other's faults, and forgive anyone who offends you. Remember, the Lord forgave you, so you must forgive others.*
[14] *Above all, clothe yourselves with love, which binds us all together in perfect harmony.* [15] *And let the peace that comes from Christ rule in your hearts.*

Colossians 3:12–15A, NLT

5. According to Colossians 3:13, does God give us the option to choose who we'll forgive and who we won't? Why is God so adamant about us forgiving?

6. Verses 12 and 14 highlight godly traits that we need to put on like clothing. What are the traits and where do we get them? How strong are these traits in your life right now?

LIFE PRINCIPLE

God flat-out commands forgiveness but it's for our benefit. Forgiveness helps maintain harmony in our relationships. It also creates deep peace and joy in the lives of the two captives it sets free—your offender and you! Festering wounds and unforgiveness keep you both in bondage. Proverbs 11:17 explains, *Your kindness will reward you, but your cruelty will destroy you* (NLT).

GENUINE FORGIVENESS

You may be ready to walk out of this study right now. You feel angry, hurt, betrayed, and here we are suggesting that you forgive and work toward trusting your husband again. You might be wondering, *Where on earth is God in all of this?*

[11] *What's going on here? Is God out to lunch? Nobody's tending the store.* [12] *The wicked get by with everything; they have it made,* [13] *I've been stupid to play by the rules; what has it gotten me?* [14] *A long run of bad luck, that's what—a slap in the face every time I walk out the door.*

PSALM 73: 11-14, THE MESSAGE

It sounds like the psalmist was screaming: "Life's just not fair!"

LEADER: *Give group members some individual time with God to respond to question 7. Offer that anyone who wants to share with the group what she wrote may do so.*

7. Isn't it comforting to see others, especially in the Bible, vent their frustrations to God? God welcomes our wrestling with Him. Write down some of the frustrations you are experiencing right now. Be honest; the psalmist sure was.

Forgive us our sins, just as we have forgiven those who have sinned against us.

MATTHEW 6:12, HCSB

Few of us have thought about what this line from the Lord's Prayer really means. Does God really forgive us in the same way we forgive others?

God has forgiven us, and He continues to forgive us. He doesn't "constantly accuse us." He "has removed our sins as far away from us as the east is from the west" (Psalm 103:9,12, NLT). *He doesn't keep any records.* How unlike us! That's why we need God's power. As we forgive others, we don't necessarily trigger God's forgiveness for us, but we do show Him that His forgiveness is real in our lives.

8. What are the implications for your husband and for your relationship if you don't keep a record of your his sins and if you separate who he is from the sin that entrapped him?

I CAN'T DO THIS!

LIFE PRINCIPLE
The truth is that you can't forgive on your own; you're going to need to lean into God and allow His supernatural power to overwhelm you.

³ For though we live in the world, we do not wage war as the world does. ⁴ The weapons we fight with are not the weapons of the world. On the contrary, they have divine power to demolish strongholds. ⁵ We demolish arguments and every pretension that sets itself up against the knowledge of God, and we take captive every thought to make it obedient to Christ.

2 CORINTHIANS 10:3-5, NIV

9. Think of your relational and personal issues as a large stronghold. What's walling you in right now? Verse 4 says that God has already provided the divinely powerful weapons, so what do we need to do to demolish our strongholds?

When someone seeks your forgiveness, you have an obligation to grant forgiveness and extend mercy—even if the person has sinned against you repeatedly in severe ways.

Even if that person wrongs you seven times a day and each time turns again and asks forgiveness, you must forgive.

LUKE 17:4, NLT

EMBRACING THE TRUTH – 20 MINUTES

Meaningful forgiveness demands thought and planning. Forgiveness is the willingness to search for new solutions—neither yours nor his but one that's mutually acceptable.

FIVE IMPORTANT STEPS IN FORGIVENESS

LEADER: *Be sure to cover all "Five Steps in Forgiveness." You may want to put these on PowerPoint slide or a flip chart. As you review each of the five steps, invite group discussion.*

STEP 1: SET ASIDE THE PAST OFFENSES

The person wounded must forgive with an act of the will, giving time to work through feelings and experience healing. We must choose not to be held captive by the past.

[God promises:] For I will forgive their wrongdoing and never again remember their sin.
JEREMIAH 31:34, HCSB

No, dear brothers and sisters, I have not achieved it, but I focus on this one thing: Forgetting the past and looking forward to what lies ahead.
PHILIPPIANS 3:13, NLT

1. How often do you find yourself replaying the moment you found out about your husband's struggle? What emotions tend to surface when your mind focuses on the past?

2. What do you see as the main barrier to forgiving your husband—relinquishing the right to get even or punishing him for his offenses?

LIFE PRINCIPLE
You'll need to keep your focus on the hope in Christ that lies ahead for you. Pray and continue to ask God to supernaturally erase the pain from your heart and mind and to take away your desire for retaliation.

STEP 2: Meditate on the radical truths of Scripture

The word of God is living and active and sharper than any two-edged sword, and piercing as far as the division of soul and spirit, of both joints and marrow, and able to judge the thoughts and intentions of the heart.

HEBREWS 4:12, NASB

3. According to Hebrews 4:12, what are the benefits of hearing from God through Scripture and in prayer?

[157] Many persecute and trouble, yet I have not swerved from your laws. [158] Seeing these traitors makes me sick at heart, because they care nothing for your word. [159] **See how I love your commandments, Lord. Give back my life because of your unfailing love.** *[160] The very essence of your words is truth; all your just regulations will stand forever.*

PSALM 119:157-160, NLT

4. Don't you want your life back? Spend time reflecting on the highlighted verse 15. Repeat this verse 10 times quietly to yourself. Each day this week think back on this verse.

STEP 3: Give our hurts to God

[17] Never pay back evil with more evil. Do things in such a way that everyone can see you are honorable. [18] Do all that you can to live in peace with everyone. [19] Dear friends, never take revenge. Leave that to the righteous anger of God. For the Scriptures say, "I will take revenge; I will pay them back," says the LORD.

ROMANS 12:17-19, NLT

5. According to Romans 12, how does God want us to respond to those who have wronged us or hurt us? (See also 1 Peter 2:21-23.) Why is God so much more qualified to avenge us?

6. As you hold your stake, pray quietly and release your hurts to God. Ask God to forgive any bitterness or spirit of retaliation. Surrender it all to God in this moment. While driving the stake in the ground ask God to help you *not* to pull the stake up again.

STEP 4: PRAY FOR YOUR HUSBAND

The power to wish your husband well rather than harm is clearly from God, and it illustrates a key hallmark that forgiveness has occurred.

[Jesus' teaching:] [27] *But I say to you who listen: Love your enemies, do good to those who hate you,* [28] *bless those who curse you, pray for those who mistreat you.*

LUKE 6:27-28, HCSB

7. What do you think is likely to happen in your attitude as you continue to pray for your husband? What are some other ways that we can bless our husbands even though we don't necessarily feel like it (see Luke 6:27-28 and also 1 Peter 3:8-9)?

STEP 5: SERVE AS A WILLING CHANNEL OF GOD'S GRACE

[Instead of taking revenge, Jesus instructs us ...] [20] *If your enemies are hungry, feed them. If they are thirsty, give them something to drink. In doing this, you will heap burning coals of shame on their head.* [21] *Don't let evil conquer you, but conquer evil by doing good.*

ROMANS 12:20-21, NLT

[13] *Now may the God of hope fill you with all joy and peace in believing, so that you may overflow with hope by the power of the Holy Spirit.* [14] *Now, my brothers, I myself am convinced about you that you also are full of goodness, filled with all knowledge, and able to instruct one another.*

ROMANS 15:13-14, HCSB

8. Why are we so dependent upon God to empower us to "conquer evil by doing good," to "overflow with hope," to comfort and "instruct one another"? Discuss the state of your spiritual vitality: Are you running on empty, filled to overflowing, or in the messy middle?

CONNECTING – 20 MINUTES

A WORD FROM RENEE

"I knew that Clay was truly repenting and asking for my forgiveness. So I gave it when he asked. However, in the days and months that followed I didn't know what to do with the doubt swimming in my head and heart. I was afraid. What if he falls to this sin again? I can remember him leaving to go back on tour, and I would be consumed with questions such as:

'Is there a supermodel sitting by him on the airplane?'

'Did he see any inappropriate magazines while he was in the airport?'

'Did he watch something on TV when he was in the hotel room?'

"The questions circled through my mind and made me bitter. My anger and fear spilled over to our two little girls. They didn't do anything wrong, yet they were catching my feelings of insecurity and my doubt in my husband. I needed peace! I wanted peace! I wanted to trust, but I didn't know if that was possible."

FEAR! It all stems from fear—of the unknown, of failure, of loss. We're not in control of this situation and as women, we're not comfortable residing in this state of the unknown.

LEADER: Use "Connecting" to deepen relationships within the group and to help each woman connect with God in a more open and personal way. Encourage group members to be completely honest about their feelings about praying for and forgiving their husbands. Invite volunteers to read the letters.

We must learn to use words that don't cast blame or create accusations.

Everyone enjoys a fitting reply; it is wonderful to say the right thing at the right time!

PROVERBS 15:23, NLT

1. How regularly do you discuss your husband's struggle with him? What's tone of voice do you intend to use? How do you think your questions sound to your husband?"

LEADER: Allow group members a couple of minutes on their own to respond to question 2. Invite anyone who would like to share what she wrote with the group to do so. Repeat this for question 5.

---

2. How often do you wrestle with doubt? Write down examples of times you've doubted your husband. Ask God to open doors for you to discuss your doubts with him. (Example: I doubt my husband when he travels. Is he being faithful to me on business trips?)

Rebuilding Trust

Forgiveness is not optional if we want to move toward healing and wholeness, but we also must recognize that it will take time for healing and trust to return to our hearts. We must communicate to our husbands that we have forgiven them but need time to process what has taken place in our lives and to rebuild trust in them.

Sooner or later we must come to the realization that we are not in control; God is. We cannot trust in ourselves or man; we must fully trust God. We must begin to release our fears to God. God will embrace us; He has promised. What wonderful promises He gives!

Letter from a Wife

"*You may think it strange to relate my husband's struggle with pornography to my battle with cancer, but God has given me a glimpse of my lack of control over any situation and His ultimate control over every situation. I was diagnosed with breast cancer a few years ago. After surgery, chemotherapy, and radiation, my cancer was in remission and I've now been cancer-free for a year. When I asked my doctor if I was truly cancer free, he said, 'Well, no one can make that guarantee, but for today, you are cancer free.' I thought about the weight I had placed on my husband. His sin is gone for now, but who is to say if it will never rear its head again? Who is to say if my cancer will return? Only God holds the future. He is in control. How I submit to that truth greatly impacts the level of peace in my life.*"

3. What lessons can we learn from this woman who had cancer?

[God encouraging us:] When you go through deep waters and great trouble, I will be with you. When you go through rivers of difficulty, you will not drown! When you walk through the fire of oppression, you will not be burned up; the flames will not consume you.

ISAIAH 43:2, NLT

When I Am Afraid

LEADER INSTRUCTIONS FOR THE GROUP EXPERIENCE: Play the song "When I Am Afraid" by Clay Crosse from the CD David—Ordinary Man—Extraordinary Man, Discovery House Music. You can also purchase the song as a download file. Set up a CD/ MP3 player before the meeting and cue the song.

4. What words or phrases from the song hit close to home for you? How so?

5. You've already listed some of your fears in question 2. Take a few minutes on your own now to list the desires of your heart for yourself, your marriage, and your family legacy. When you leader calls you back together, share your list with the group.

Be encouraged, my friend. You and others in the group can feel protected, secure, cherished, and special with your husband again. Most definitely you will feel that way with God.

- Pray that God will give your husband compassion and tenderness toward you.
- Pray that God will return to you the security that has been taken away.

> LEADER: *You may want to spend some time in group prayer, but avoid making any woman feel that she must pray aloud.*

MY PRAYER NEEDS
(List your emotional as well as spiritual needs.)

MY GROUP'S PRAYER NEEDS

TAKING IT HOME

A CHALLENGE FROM RENEE

In 1998 God allowed vocal problems to get Clay's attention about his struggle. He went to a vocal instructor, Chris Beatty, in Nashville to get help with his problem. I can remember how he described his singing difficulties. "It feels like when I sing, someone has a hand on my throat." We know now it was God's hand getting his attention.

Mr. Beatty listened as Clay told him about the singing problem. Interestingly he had a different remedy for Clay. He asked Clay: "What are you reading in God's Word?" "How's your prayer life?" "How is your relationship with Renee?" "Clay, are you a man of God?" These questions shocked Clay. After all, he was there to get his voice fixed, but the Holy Spirit of God was at work. Clay hadn't known Chris 10 minutes, and he found himself crying in Chris's office. The questions he asked were basic "Christianity 101" questions we as believers should be able to answer at any time. God was softening Clay's heart and opening his eyes to the reality of his need to truly recommit his life to Him.

ACTION: I encourage you to pray a "Chris Beatty" into your husband's life. Having a strong man of God in your husband's life is a wonderful gift from God. It can be emotionally draining and virtually impossible for a wife to take on the pressure of being her husband's accountability partner and spiritual guide. God knows how important this man was in the life of my husband, and God wants His best for your husband as well.

If your husband could join with a few other men in going through the Serendipity study *The Secret Seductress*, he and the others would find themselves on an amazing healing journey.

JOURNALING ACTION: Take some time to write out your heart's desires for yourself, your husband, your marriage, and your family legacy on the journal page that follows.

QUESTIONS TO TAKE TO MY HEART

* How willing am I to trust my husband again? (Be honest and answer this question, right where you are today.) What are my deepest fears about trusting my husband again?

* Am I still harboring unforgiveness? If so, what hurt or fear sits behind my unforgiveness? What fears am I still holding onto rather than trusting the goodness of God's heart toward me?

Take at least one of the following Scriptures to meditate on and memorize this week. Write it on a card and place it in a prominent spot (e.g. in your car, on a mirror, on the kitchen fridge).

So we say with confidence, "The Lord is my helper; I will not be afraid. What can man do to me?"
HEBREWS 13:6, NIV

[3] When I am afraid. I will put my trust in you. [4] I praise God for what he has promised. I trust in God, so why should I be afraid? What can mere mortals do to me?
PSALM 56:3-4, NASB

[7] But blessed is the man who trusts God, the woman who sticks with God. [8] They're like trees replanted in Eden, putting down roots near the rivers.
JEREMIAH 17: 7-8A, THE MESSAGE

[7] They do not fear bad news; they confidently trust the LORD to care for them. [8] They are confident and fearless and can face their foes triumphantly
PSALM 112:7-8, NLT

The one who understands a matter finds success, and the one who trusts in the LORD will be happy.
PROVERBS 16:20, HCSB

We know that God causes all things to work together for good to those who love God, to those who are called according to His purpose.
ROMANS 8:28, NASB

[38] I am convinced that nothing can ever separate us from God's love. Neither death nor life, neither angels nor demons, neither our fears for today nor our worries about tomorrow—not even the powers of hell can separate us from God's love. [39] No power in the sky above or in the earth below— indeed, nothing in all creation will ever be able to separate us from the love of God that is revealed in Christ Jesus our Lord.
ROMANS. 8:38-39, NLT

You may also want to search the Scriptures for yourself. Ask God to show you in His Word passages that meet you right where you are. You might purchase a Bible concordance, a topical Bible, or an in-depth study Bible to help you search for passages. Online tools are available at *BibleStudyTools.net*, *BibleGateway.com*, *BibleCrosswalk.com*, or *LifeWay.com*.

NOTES:

1. Adapted from Ramon Presson, *Radical Reconciliation* (Nashville: Serendipity by LifeWay, 2007), from the Picking Up the Pieces series.

DREAMS FOR MYSELF, MY HUSBAND, AND MY MARRIAGE

I'm Done with This

Getting Started - 15 minutes

In previous sessions we revealed our hurt, realized that the issue we're dealing with is not our fault, and addressed our deep feelings of anger and resentment. Then we explored forgiveness. Forgiveness is vital, but not easy. Spend just a few moments discussing what group members learned as they completed the assignment from last week.

LEADER INSTRUCTIONS FOR THE GROUP EXPERIENCE: Have a TV/DVD player set up ready to play any "Challenge" or "Endurance Exercise" clip from the television show "Survivor." You can rent DVDs from the Survivor Series at a video store or watch clips online at www.cbs.com/primetime/survivor16.

Survival Challenge

Let's kick into survivor mode for a moment. Think back to the television program "Survivor." Its motto is "Outwit, Outplay, Outlast." At some point in the season they have an exercise in endurance. Something that seems easy to do, but this is where the will to win must kick in.

LEADER: Play the short Endurance or Challenge clip, and then facilitate the following "endurance challenge." Conclude this activity with the questions that follow.

INSTRUCTIONS: We aren't going to leave this room and head to an island in the middle of nowhere, but pretend for a moment we're in a "challenge" within the group.

Challenge 1: Have each group member stand and bend one leg at the knee. See how long each one can stand without putting her foot down.

Challenge 2: Have each group member start off by holding a book in one hand. After a few seconds, add another book. Continue until there is only one person left holding her stack of books.

1. How would you rate yourself as far as physical endurance—high, medium, or low? How about your emotional/spiritual endurance?

2. How has going through this struggle with your husband tested your endurance?

3. How strong is your willpower to stay with the challenge? If some of you need a fresh infusion of God's vision for your marriage and family or a boost of encouragement to persevere, take a few minutes to pray for one another

A WORD FROM RENEE

"Soon after Clay's confession I remember thinking to myself: He asked God to forgive him, and he asked for my forgiveness, so everything will be OK now. This was quite an unrealistic bubble I chose to live in.

"A few weeks later I saw him noticing an attractive woman while we were at dinner. I asked him why he was looking at her. I thought that we had this problem fixed. How could he hurt me again? He must be the most insensitive man on the planet, I thought. We left the restaurant and I was furious. I told him it hurt way too much to continue in that cycle. I didn't want to leave him; I just didn't want to get hurt anymore.

"Looking back, I can see that my expectations for him to 'get over' his problem with lust were not exactly fair. I expected him to be perfect from that moment on, though we all know that no one except Jesus lived a perfect life on earth.

"We were able to talk that evening, and he did apologize for what had taken place earlier at the restaurant. 'Can I be patient with him?' I wondered. My answer: 'I really don't know.' I knew I would have to ask for God's help.

"You may be in this place as well. Not knowing if you can continue on this path or if you even want to. But before you make up your mind to just try to escape the pain, stay open to hear from God during this study."

Objectives for this Session

- Address our tendency to avoid or escape pain in our lives.

- Examine our hearts and determine what it takes to persevere.

- Bring to light the spirit of longsuffering and the work of redemption that God wants to pour out on us.

- Use a journal exercise to help us adopt an attitude of longsuffering and perseverance.

Discovering the Truth – 35 Minutes

LEADER: *In "Discovering the Truth" the group will begin to deal with some mountains that may now seem insurmountable. Be sure to leave time for the "Embracing the Truth" and "Connecting" segments. Review the "Reclaiming Your Life Together" map and note the group's progress.*

Reclaiming Your Life Together

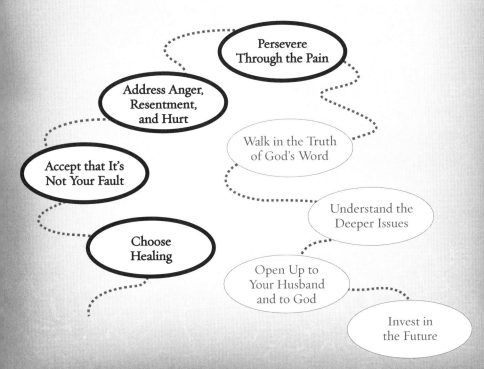

Persevere Through the Pain

Address Anger, Resentment, and Hurt

Walk in the Truth of God's Word

Accept that It's Not Your Fault

Understand the Deeper Issues

Choose Healing

Open Up to Your Husband and to God

Invest in the Future

OPENING PRAYER

THERE'S PAIN IN PERSEVERANCE

Perseverance sounds noble, but we seldom ask, "Where can I sign up for another chance to endure a difficult life struggle?"

LIFE PRINCIPLE

It is one thing to say you forgive and a totally different thing to keep forgiving and persevering in a relationship in which you've been hurt and in a time when you're still shaky about the future.

The Woman's Study Bible explains, "'Perseverance' is the biblical term used to describe Christians who faithfully endure and remain steadfast in the face of opposition, attack, and discouragement. Those who focus on Jesus can bear up under any load. Perseverance involves *patience*—the ability to endure without complaint and with calmness. Perseverance also includes *persistence* in accomplishing goals and *permanence* for a lifetime of commitment."[1]

1. What's honestly going on in your mind and heart when you read: "Those who focus on Jesus can bear up under any load"?

2. As you've dealt with the pain, how often have you considered that it might be easier to just walk away—to be released from your commitment of "for better or worse"?

[17] *I gave up on life altogether. I've forgotten what the good life is like.* [18] *I said to myself, "This is it. I'm finished. GOD is a lost cause."* [19] *I'll never forget the trouble, the utter lostness, the taste of ashes, the poison I've swallowed.* [20] *I remember it all—oh, how well I remember—the feeling of hitting the bottom.*

LAMENTATIONS 3:17-20, THE MESSAGE

3. In what ways can you relate to Jeremiah's feelings as he cries out to the Lord in Lamentations 3:17-20? According to Lamentations 3:17-20, what are some lies that become deeply embedded into the wounds in our hearts and can lead us to despair?

A Word from Renee

"When Clay asked me to forgive him, he told me that he hadn't physically committed adultery but that in his mind he had many times. He went on to say that he knew what God's Word said about this. As a wife, this crushed my spirit. I knew what God's Word said about the subject too. It left me feeling sick; I just wanted to throw up. But I could see that Clay wasn't running from this. He was facing up to his sin and asking for forgiveness. He was broken, but ... so was I."

[Jesus raised the bar for us:] 27 You have heard the commandment that says, "You must not commit adultery." 28 But I say, anyone who even looks at a woman with lust has already committed adultery with her in his heart.

MATTHEW 5:27-28, NLT

4. Do you believe the Bible gives you an approved option to leave your marriage because of the mental or physical adultery? If people really knew the story, do you think they would blame you for leaving?

It's easy to berate, threaten, or beat our husbands over their heads with verses like Matthew 5:27-28, but these actions only show that we've not yet forgiven from the heart or that we've given up on our resolve to give mercy rather than to punish or retaliate.

The Bible gives only two grounds for which God permits divorce: abandonment and physical adultery (at least the ongoing pattern of sex with others).

Letter from a Hurting Wife

"My husband has struggled with pornography since he was 12 years old. He has lost two jobs, and I am afraid that it will soon be three. He looks at pornography on the computer at work. The first two times I forgave him and tried to move on, but I realize this time that he is not transparent. I always have to pry out of him if he is having lust problems. I feel very tired. I just found out that he has been looking again. At first, he said it was my fault. I am ready to leave him because I just don't trust him or think that he is really fighting to do what God wants or what is best for our family. Please pray for me."

The Power of Staying in the Pain

When we hurt, it's only natural to protect ourselves and shield ourselves from pain. Self-preservation is a core belief in our world. "The world is not comfortable with commitment ... The children of God are called to a life of commitment to God and each other. To faith, virtue, and knowledge, the believer is required to add self-control and perseverance ... The promise is that those who endure and persevere in overcoming evil will be greatly rewarded with God's blessings both now and in eternity."[2]

[8] *The one who sows to his own flesh will from the flesh reap corruption, but the one who sows to the Spirit will from the Spirit reap eternal life.* [9] *Let us not lose heart in doing good, for in due time we will reap if we do not grow weary.*

GALATIANS 6:8-9, NASB

6. How does the Bible turn the world's perspective on self-preservation upside down in Galatians 6:8-9? What happens when we stay in our in pain rather than escaping or avoiding the difficult, hurtful things?

7. Losing heart is the opposite of persevering. In some of life's trials we don't lose heart or grow weary, but in others we barely hang on. What do you think makes the difference?

The relationship of Hosea and his wife Gomer epitomizes betrayal and unfaithfulness and yet ends up reflecting forgiveness and restoration. It truly is a "God story."

In a time when God's chosen people defiantly turned away from Him and pursued idolatry, God called Hosea to a strange and difficult role of demonstrating the painful relationship between God and His people, his bride. He was commanded to marry Gomer (Hosea 1:2).

"Gomer conducted her harlotry in a shamefully flagrant manner. ... the consequences of her actions, especially the agony she caused her husband and children ... were the unavoidable realities of her selfish behavior. Gomer sought her own enjoyment so irresponsibly that she ultimately ended up in some sort of bondage from which she had to be redeemed (Hosea 3:1-3). As Hosea paid the price for her and took her back to himself, he restored her as his wife after a preliminary period of discipline to help her direct her life afresh to the vows she had made to Hosea in marriage."[3]

The story of Hosea and Gomer is meant to illustrate a love that cannot be explained— the mysterious love from God that redeems, forgives, reconciles, and restores no matter what. By contrast, the world would say: "You don't deserve to be treated that way. Get out while you can."

8. What hurts and issues would you imagine Hosea faced in obeying God? How does your husband's struggle affect your feelings of shame, humiliation, and self-image? Discuss how these feelings affect your relationship.

9. Extreme love—tough and tender—finally broke through Gomer's unfaithful spirit. How confident are you really that God wants to redeem and restore your marriage? How confident are you that you'll eventually break through to your husband's heart?

LIFE PRINCIPLE
We need to stay in our pain long enough to allow God to use our suffering for our good and the good of others.

Embracing the Truth – 20 Minutes

Developing Longsuffering: "An Optimistic Waiting"

Unfortunately, there's no shortcut to develop longsuffering. "Longsuffering encompasses patience, endurance, steadfastness, and forbearance. It is an active response to opposition, not a passive resignation to the inevitable. An important word in both Hebrew and Greek, 'longsuffering' is an attribute of God ... a fruit of the Holy Spirit ... and an attitude all women should desire to reflect in their lives."[4]

[1] Let us also lay aside every encumbrance and the sin which so easily entangles us, and let us run with endurance the race that is set before us, [2] fixing our eyes on Jesus, the author and perfecter of faith, who for the joy set before Him endured the cross, despising the shame, and has sat down at the right hand of the throne of God. [3] For consider Him who has endured such hostility by sinners against Himself, so that you will not grow weary and lose heart.

HEBREWS 12:1-3, NASB

[29] [God] gives strength to the weary and increases the power of the weak. [30] Even youths grow tired and weary, and young men stumble and fall; [31] but those who hope in the LORD will renew their strength. They will soar on wings like eagles; they will run and not grow weary, they will walk and not be faint.

ISAIAH 40:29-31, NASB

1. God has set your own unique race before you (Hebrews 12:1). From Hebrews 12:1-3 and Isaiah 40:29-31, identify as many ways as possible that we can tap into God and develop more longsuffering.

2. What can we learn from Jesus' example? What was His motivation for staying in the pain and enduring the cross?

[God speaking:] I will lead the blind by ways they have not known, along unfamiliar paths I will guide them; I will turn the darkness into light before them and make the rough places smooth. These are the things I will do; I will not forsake them.

ISAIAH 42:16, NIV

3. In what ways do you feel "blind" as you follow God on the path to redemption? What's your deepest concern or fear about taking the "unfamiliar path" with God (Isaiah 42:16)?

4. What's the worst thing that could happen as you loosen your grip and allow God to take you back into your pain and the darkness in your marriage? What could this group do to help you risk the next step you know you need to take?

LIFE PRINCIPLE

More than anything, the healing journey requires us to deeply trust God. Healing the wounds in our innermost being will lead us down paths we never could have imagined.

BITTER OR BETTER?

[3] We can rejoice, too, when we run into problems and trials, for we know that they help us develop endurance. [4] And endurance develops strength of character, and character strengthens our confident hope of salvation. [5] And this hope will not lead to disappointment. For we know how dearly God loves us, because he has given us the Holy Spirit to fill our hearts with his love.

ROMANS 5:3-5, NLT

Problems and suffering don't automatically make you stronger or better. It's the way you respond to suffering that determines if you become better or bitter.

"God has provided his grace to soothe in times of hurting—refusing that grace creates an inner environment where bitterness can grow. Every woman at some point in her life experiences being wronged by another. She then chooses whether to forgive or to dwell upon the wrongdoing until she becomes bitter. ... Bitterness defiles all those it touches, starting with the one who is bitter, but extending to other relationships ...

"Bitterness can have far-reaching, long-lasting, and self-destructive effects. A bitter woman must first turn to Christ ... Once she has accepted His forgiveness, then she is not only able, but commanded to forgive others... One very practical way to do that is to replace bitterness with love ... especially by showing love to the one who has wronged her."[5]

5. How much bitterness has wormed its way into your heart? In what ways, if any, are you feeling impacts—physical, mental, emotional—of holding onto bitterness?

Pray and invite the Holy Spirit to produce such fruit in your life. Now, commit to memorize one of the three following passages of Scripture.

⁷ Be silent before the LORD and wait expectantly for Him; do not be agitated by one who prospers in his way, by the man who carries out evil plans. ⁸ Refrain from anger and give up your rage; do not be agitated—it can only bring harm. ⁹ For evildoers will be destroyed, but those who put their hope in the LORD will inherit the land.

PSALM 37:7-9, HCSB

²⁵ The LORD is good to those who wait for Him, to the person who seeks Him. ²⁶ It is good to wait quietly for deliverance from the LORD.

LAMENTATIONS 3:25-26, NLT

CONNECTING – 20 MINUTES

LEADER: This "Connecting" experience will be challenging. The decision to forgive and persevere may be difficult for some (or all). Asking group members to put on spiritual binoculars and look way out into the future will also be difficult, but it's necessary for them to see that there's a lot at stake.

In any drama there's a crisis point. This is also true in real-life drama. God is waiting on your response to this crisis in your life. There are several options for you:

- Forgive, persevere, and allow God to redeem.
- Just stick it out and let the bitterness spread.
- Take the escape hatch and walk out of the relationship.

Carefully consider your choices and the long-term impacts of your choice. One way or the other, your marriage *will* leave a legacy in your family and in the world. Your legacy will have ramifications for generations.

"Our task is not to showcase perfect families within our communities but rather to allow an unbelieving world to see ordinary families struggling with real issues, yet finding strength and wisdom in a loving, sufficient Savior."[5]

LEADER INSTRUCTIONS FOR THE GROUP EXPERIENCE: Secure the CD Live at the Door *or download a copy of the song "Legacy" by Nichole Nordeman. Set up a CD/MP3 player and play the song for the group.*

---

1. In her song "Legacy" Nichole Nordeman sings to God, "I want to leave a legacy. How will they remember me? Did I choose to love? Did I point to You enough to make a mark on things?" As you listen to the song, write down some thoughts and feelings about the legacy you want to leave.

God never promised us that this life would be easy. However, He did promise never to leave us. God is as close as your breath no matter how tough life gets.

[1] Do not be afraid, for I have ransomed you. I have called you by name; you are mine. [2] When you go through deep waters, I will be with you. When you go through rivers of difficulty, you will not drown. When you walk through the fire of oppression, you will not be burned up; the flames will not consume you. [3] For I am the Lord, your God, the Holy One of Israel, your Savior.

ISAIAH 43:1B-3A, NLT

2. What assurances does God give in Isaiah 43:1-3 for the various fears you might face moving forward? Which of these assurances gives you the greatest comfort? Explain.

Jesus invites you to enter into His rest. Stop and take a moment to breathe Isaiah 43:1-3 and Matthew 11:28-30 into your life.

[Jesus invites us:] [28] "Are you tired? Worn out? Burned out on religion? Come to me. Get away with me and you'll recover your life. I'll show you how to take a real rest. [29] Walk with me and work with me—watch how I do it. Learn the unforced rhythms of grace. I won't lay anything heavy or ill-fitting on you. [30] Keep company with me and you'll learn to live freely and lightly."

MATTHEW 11:28-30, THE MESSAGE

3. What would you have to change in your heart and mind to enable you to rest in following God's "unfamiliar path," accepting Jesus' offer to walk with Him, work with Him, and learn the unforced rhythms of grace?

LEADER: *Provide a 3x5-inch card for each woman to take home. "Taking It Home" gives instructions for writing an affirmation on the card. Close by praying for key needs in the group.*

MY PRAYER AND SUPPORT NEEDS:

MY GROUP'S PRAYER AND SUPPORT NEEDS:

LEADER: *Emphasize that the choice to persevere is an ongoing process. Encourage group members to be patient and continue to take steps forward. Remind them that you and your team of leaders are available any time they need to talk or just hang out with a caring friend. Review "Taking It Home."*

TAKING IT HOME

SHARING AFFIRMATION IN YOUR GROUP

Sometimes we don't realize what a toll the messages we are bombarded with take on our self-esteem. Everyone needs to feel worth. Spend a few moments affirming the other women in your group. On a 3x5-inch card write a word of affirmation directed toward the women in your group. Put the card in your book and take it with you to the next gathering.

QUESTIONS TO TAKE TO MY HEART

✳ What if I feel like I can never trust my husband again—what will I do?

QUESTIONS TO TAKE TO GOD

✳ God, what do You want to say to me about my wounds/burdens? What do You want to say to me about joining You on the unfamiliar path?

JOURNAL EXERCISE

In your journal write your honest responses to these questions. Give considerable thought to your answers, and pray for God's wisdom and discernment as you write.

1. Think about your future with your husband, children, extended family, and friends. How might the choices you're making during this difficult season impact each of them?
2. Are you able to share your journey with any of the people you thought about above?
3. If someone were on the outside looking at how you're handling this trial, how would he or she respond to what's happening?
4. Think about the repercussions of giving up on your marriage. Consider holidays, special events, weddings, birthdays, and school functions. Realize that what may seem easy in the short run will bring a lifetime of awkwardness and difficult consequences.
5. Think about the legacy you would leave if God redeems your marriage. In Christ your marriage will serve as a living testimony of God's grace and power. Write down what you'd like to see God do in and through your marriage and in the life of your husband.

NOTES:

1. *The Woman's Study Bible* (Nashville: Thomas Nelson, Inc., 1995).
2-5. Ibid.

MY LEGACY

RISING FROM GROUND ZERO

GETTING STARTED - 10 MINUTES

LEADER INSTRUCTIONS FOR THE GROUP EXPERIENCE: Collect the 3x5-inch cards that the ladies wrote an affirmation on at home this week. Be sure to bring extra cards for those who did not bring a card and give them time to write something affirming on the card.

When instructed by your leader, pull a card other than the one you wrote from the pile of affirmation cards. Go around the group with each person reading the affirmation aloud to the group. When you're finished, take the card you selected home as an ongoing reminder and encouragement.

OPENING PRAYER

Yes, Lord, we are aware that there's an enemy that seeks to destroy, but we're also aware of Your mighty right hand that will save us and the husbands You've given us. Help us rise from this moment to embrace the hope that You are ready to pour into our lives. Walk with us and show us Your ways. Keep us mindful of the variety of counsel that we may be receiving. Lord, give us wisdom and discernment to know if counsel is coming from You or the world. Thanks for joining us today. Amen.

OBJECTIVES FOR THIS SESSION

- Learn to put your trust in God for healing.
- Begin to understand your part in the healing and rebuilding process.
- Embrace the refining process God desires to see take place in your life.
- Prepare yourself to rise up from the ashes in your life and find a way through.
- Allow this life challenge to strengthen you in your own spiritual journey.

DISCOVERING THE TRUTH – 20 MINUTES

RECLAIMING YOUR LIFE TOGETHER

Our journey remains very challenging.

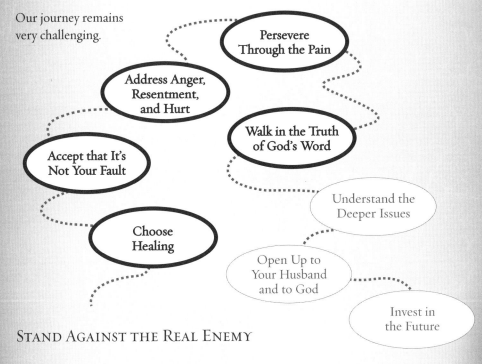

- Persevere Through the Pain
- Address Anger, Resentment, and Hurt
- Walk in the Truth of God's Word
- Accept that It's Not Your Fault
- Understand the Deeper Issues
- Choose Healing
- Open Up to Your Husband and to God
- Invest in the Future

STAND AGAINST THE REAL ENEMY

Do you remember where you were on September 11, 2001 when the World Trade Center towers were attacked by terrorists? News coverage referred to the site of the Twin Towers as "Ground Zero." Something had taken place on this spot that would forever change the shape and course of our future. The U.S. President proclaimed that we would take on this "Axis of Evil" that seeks to destroy us. An amazing resolve rose up across the land. We'd taken a devastating hit, but we stood together against the enemy.

In this group, we've also been devastated by an attack from our enemy—the real enemy, Satan. He is well aware of our husbands' vulnerabilities … and ours.

1. You may feel like a bomb blew and "leveled" the life you've carefully built. As with the events of September 11, what are some fallout events you've faced throughout your life?

^{10} *Be strong in the Lord and in his mighty power.* ^{11} *Put on the full armor of God so that you can take your stand against the devil's schemes.* ^{12} *For our struggle is not against flesh and blood, but against the rulers, against the authorities, against the powers of this dark world and against the spiritual forces of evil in the heavenly realms.*

EPHESIANS 6:10-12, NIV

It's natural to see a person who's hurt or wronged you, especially your husband, as uncaring, malicious, and disgusting—in short, your enemy.

2. According to Ephesians 6:11-12, who's the real villain in our lives and marriages? What schemes do you think he's used against your husband to drag him down?

3. What schemes have you noticed the "spiritual forces of evil" using against you and your husband to undermine or ruin your marriage and your legacy?

^{13} *Be alert, stand firm in the faith, be brave and strong.* ^{14} *Your every action must be done with love.*

1 CORINTHIANS 16:13-14, HCSB

Stand firm against him [the Devil], and be strong in your faith. Remember that your Christian brothers and sisters all over the world are going through the same kind of suffering you are.

1 PETER 5:9, NLT

4. Alertness, faith, courage, love are key traits we need to resist enemy attacks (1 Peter 5:9; 1 Corinthians 16:13-14;). Discuss practical ways to apply these traits in your situation.

Ladies, we have a decision to make here: Will we stand together in this group to proclaim our resolve and unite against this enemy that seeks to destroy our husbands, our security, our families, and our witness to a broken world?

LIFE PRINCIPLE

Jesus promised that we *would* experience trouble and suffering in this world. It's not the problems, but the way you respond to difficult, even gut-wrenching situations that defines who you are, the path for your life, and the legacy you will leave.

Read aloud in unison these words from 2 Corinthians 4:8-9,11,16 from the HCSB:

8 We are pressured in every way but not crushed; we are perplexed but not in despair; 9 we are persecuted but not abandoned; we are struck down but not destroyed. ... 11 For we who live are always given over to death because of Jesus, so that Jesus' life may also be revealed in our mortal flesh. ... 16 Therefore we do not give up; even though our outer person is being destroyed, our inner person is being renewed day by day.

5. Which of these words from 2 Corinthians 4 describe your life and feelings right now? Where do you think Jesus is in all of this mess?

6. Will you choose to let this moment define your life or rise from "Ground Zero?" How ready are you now to extend forgiveness and to declare your resolve to battle the spiritual and cultural enemies that seek to destroy your marriage?

EMBRACING THE TRUTH – 35 MINUTES

LEADER: *"Embracing the Truth" continues the discussion of forgiveness and resolve as the keys to true freedom. Lead group members to see this choice: Do we withhold forgiveness from the men who hurt us and walk away? Or, do we forgive them and allow God to work through us to bring about restoration and renewed intimacy with our husbands and with Him?*

HOW TO STAND WITH YOUR HUSBAND IN BATTLE

It's not always easy, but God's Word, the Bible, gives us many practical helps so we can take steps into forgiveness and reconciliation. Colossians 2:6 states clearly the kind of faith that's required: *"Therefore as you have received Christ Jesus the Lord, so walk in Him"* (NASB).

FREEDOM. The very word sounds so inviting and peaceful. We want to be free from the pain in our lives. We also need to be free from bitterness, broken relationships, and the power of the Villain in our stories. Let's help each other learn a new path to freedom.

In prayer there is a connection between what God does and what you do. You can't get forgiveness from God, for instance, without also forgiving others.

MATTHEW 6:14, THE MESSAGE

[12] Since God chose you to be the holy people he loves, you must clothe yourselves with tenderhearted mercy, kindness, humility, gentleness, and patience. [13] Make allowance for each other's faults, and forgive anyone who offends you. Remember, the Lord forgave you, so you must forgive others.

COLOSSIANS 3:12-13, NLT

1. What two important truths in Colossians 3:12-13, sit behind God's requirement that we forgive? What are some ways unforgiveness can keep us and our husbands in bondage?

LIFE PRINCIPLE

Remember, forgiveness does not minimize or excuse the offense. Instead, it ceases to define the offender by his sin or failure. Be deeply thankful that God forgives and does not define you by your worst or repeated sins.

[6] The punishment inflicted on him by the majority is sufficient for him. [7] Now instead, you ought to forgive and comfort him, so that he will not be overwhelmed by excessive sorrow. [8] I urge you, therefore, to reaffirm your love for him. ... [10] I have forgiven in the sight of Christ for your sake, [11] in order that Satan might not outwit us. For we are not unaware of his schemes.

2 CORINTHIANS 2:6-11, NIV

2. The man Paul identified caused pain to many. What can happen if we withhold forgiveness and refuse to treat our husbands with dignity or to comfort them (verses 7,11)?

3. Discuss practical ways to "forgive and comfort." How about ways to "reaffirm your love"?

[8] All of you should be of one mind. Sympathize with each other. Love each other as brothers and sisters. Be tenderhearted, and keep a humble attitude. [9] Don't repay evil for evil. Don't retaliate with insults when people insult you. Instead, pay them back with a blessing. That is what God has called you to do, and he will bless you for it.

1 PETER 3:8-9, NLT

4. How does God's approach in 1 Peter 3:9 differ from the world's handling of offenses or evil deeds? How might your husband respond if you bless his life rather than retaliating?

It gets really tough when we have husbands who are either not Christ-followers or who don't want to submit areas of their lives to following God's ways. God gives us *uncommon wisdom* for the way we should speak and act in 2 Timothy 2:24-26 and 1 Peter 3:1-2.

24 The Lord's servant must not quarrel; instead, he must be kind to everyone, able to teach, not resentful. 25 Those who oppose him he must gently instruct, in the hope that God will grant them repentance leading them to a knowledge of the truth, 26 and that they will come to their senses and escape from the trap of the devil, who has taken them captive to do his will.

2 TIMOTHY 2:24-26, NIV

1 Likewise, wives, be subject to your own husbands so that even if some do not obey the word, they may be won without a word by the conduct of their wives—2 when they see your respectful and pure conduct.

1 PETER 3:2, ESV

5. How do you feel about the approaches outlined in 2 Timothy 2:24-26 and 1 Peter 3:1-2? Is there anything that just rubs against the grain of how you like to handle things? Discuss struggles and benefits of this approach with people in your group.

25 What this adds up to, then, is this: no more lies, no more pretense. Tell your neighbor [or husband] the truth. In Christ's body we're all connected to each other, after all. When you lie to others, you end up lying to yourself. 26 Go ahead and be angry. You do well to be angry—but don't use your anger as fuel for revenge. And don't stay angry. Don't go to bed angry. 27 Don't give the Devil that kind of foothold in your life.

EPHESIANS 4:25-27, THE MESSAGE

6. Amazingly, we're commanded in Ephesians 4 to go ahead and be angry, but not to sin in our anger. How can we drop the cover-ups and pretenses with our husbands, being open and honest, without being vengeful or sinning?

LIFE PRINCIPLE

When you forgive, you allow God to work in your life and in your husband's life. When you give a blessing instead of retaliating, you see the power of God unleashed. When you honestly share your feelings with gentleness, love, and respect, your husband won't know what hit him ... because eventually you'll touch his heart.

A WORD FROM RENEE

"In 1998 when Clay recommitted his life to God, I began to see changes. I noticed him reading his Bible. (A sight I had never seen before in our home.) And his prayers started to seem so personal and real. While I didn't have the 'ugly' sin he had confessed in my life, I knew I was far from God. Oh sure, I accepted Christ when I was a little girl, but I had done little to show a life devoted to Him.

"I didn't want Clay to run off and leave me spiritually, so I started reading the Bible too. Regardless of my first intentions, you can't open His Word and not be transformed by its truth. To be perfectly honest, some of the truth I read wasn't easy to digest. I recall a night when I didn't want Clay in the same bed with me. I was really mad! You see, I'd asked him if he thought of 'images' he'd seen when he was with me. I simply could not handle his honest answer. I left and went to sleep on the couch. I thought about opening my Bible there on the coffee table. At the same time I really didn't want to open it. I think I knew I would hear from God, and I wanted to stay in my anger a little longer. After all, didn't I have the right?

"As the night went on, God would not leave me alone. I finally gave in. I opened my Bible and read Matthew 5:43-48—you know the passage: 'Pray for your enemies.' Well as I read further into the passage, verse 44 jumped out at me: "Pray for those who spitefully use you" (NKJV). As a wife, I felt used by my husband. How could he be with me yet think of the image of another woman he'd seen in a magazine?

"I had a choice to make—stay bitter, stay on the couch, or obey God and pray for Clay. I argued with God: 'I don't want to pray for him. I'm the one who got hurt.' I asked, 'How can You require so much of me? It's not fair!' I threw a real temper fit before God; then something happened inside me. I realized how much better I felt to get that off my chest. God already knew what I was feeling so what did I have to lose by voicing my feelings? Actually it was therapeutic. It didn't change His mind though. I still heard Him say obey and trust Me or keep sleeping on the couch. I picked up my pillow and walked down the hall to our bedroom. As Clay slept, I put my hands over him and prayed for him. Sleep came easy after that. I know firsthand, there is peace in obedience to God."

Fighting for Your Husband and Your Marriage

But I say to you, love your enemies, bless those who curse you, do good to those who hate you, and pray for those who spitefully use you and persecute you.

JESUS IN MATTHEW 5:44, NKJV

7. Jesus often turns conventional wisdom on its head. Why would He ask us to do something in Matthew 5:44 that runs so counter to our feelings? What impacts would praying for our husbands have on them? On us?

Do not deprive each other of sexual relations, unless you both agree to refrain from sexual intimacy for a limited time so you can give yourselves more completely to prayer. Afterward, you should come together again so that Satan won't be able to tempt you because of your lack of self-control.

1 CORINTHIANS 7:5, NLT

8. Perhaps sexual relations with your husband is one of the last things on your mind right now. Why is the Bible so adamant about this point in 1 Corinthians 7:5? Discuss possible scenarios that could play out if you "deprive each other" sexually?

9. Merely going through the motions of the sexual act will not be fulfilling for your husband or for you; 1 Corinthians 7:5 refers to relating to one another through sex. What issues we might need to address in order to reengage sexually with our husbands?

LEADER: *Sex can be a major stumbling block for some women depending upon the depth of the hurt, the seriousness of sex addictions, and the makeup of the couple. If you sense significant struggles, be ready to refer group members to a Christian counselor or pastor experienced in dealing with sexual issues (for counselors in your area, check www.family.org or www.aacc.net).*

[Jesus speaking to the Church in Thyatira:] ²⁰ *But I have this against you, that you tolerate the woman Jezebel, who calls herself a prophetess and is teaching and seducing my servants to practice sexual immorality and to eat food sacrificed to idols.* ²¹ *I gave her time to repent, but she refuses to repent of her sexual immorality.*

REVELATION 2:20-21, ESV

10. As we see in Revelation 2:20, God is not soft on either sexual sin or spiritual/emotional unfaithfulness. What are other steps we could take so we don't "tolerate" the Jezebels or seductresses that strive to drag down our husbands?

God knows what's happened in your life. He knows that rising from "Ground Zero" can be difficult and slow, but He doesn't expect you to rebuild on your own. He has the blueprints for the reconstruction. Mediate on and discuss the following blueprints.

Unless the LORD builds the house, they labor in vain who build it; unless the LORD guards the city, the watchman keeps awake in vain.

PSALM 127:1, NASB

Humanly speaking, it is impossible. But with God everything is possible.

MATTHEW 19:26, NLT

²⁰ *Now to him who is able to do immeasurably more than all we ask or imagine, according to his power that is at work within us,* ²¹ *to him be glory in the church and in Christ Jesus throughout all generations, for ever and ever! Amen.*

EPHESIANS 3:21, NIV

CONNECTING – 25 MINUTES

LEADER: *Continue to express understanding for the difficult struggles each woman is facing. Encourage them to take their hurts, doubts, and anger to God. He welcomes and rewards those who will wrestle through issues with Him. Use the "Connecting" experience to give hope and courage to groups members.*

The Refiner's Fire

² But who will be able to endure it when he comes? Who will be able to stand and face him when he appears? For he will be like a blazing fire that refines metal, or like a strong soap that bleaches clothes. ³ He will sit like a refiner of silver, burning away the dross. He will purify the Levites, refining them like gold and silver ... (Malachi 3:2-3, NLT).

"A woman wanted to understand the process of refining silver so she visited the silversmith. She didn't tell him why she was there, but she asked him to explain the process of refining silver, which he fully described to her. But sir, she said, 'do you sit while the work of the refining is going on?' Oh yes, madam replied the silversmith; I must sit with my eye steadily fixed on the furnace, for if the time necessary for refining be exceeded in the slightest degree, the silver will be injured.

"The lady at once saw the beauty, and comfort too, of the expression 'He shall sit as a refiner and purifier of silver.' Christ sees it necessary to put His children into a furnace; His eye is steadily intent on the work of purifying and His wisdom and love are both engaged in the best manner for them. Their trials do not come at random; 'the very hairs of your head are numbered.'

"As the lady was leaving the shop, the silversmith called her back, and said he had forgotten to mention that the only way to know when the process of purifying is complete is when he sees his own image reflected in the silver."[1]

⁸ Let the whole world bless our God and loudly sing his praises. ⁹ Our lives are in his hands, and he keeps our feet from stumbling. ¹⁰ You have tested us, O God; you have purified us like silver.

PSALM 66:8-10, NLT

Look closely at the steps in the refining process.

1. **Silver is heated or put in the fire.** Do you recognize that the trial you're experiencing is placing you in God's refining fire? Has there been another time that you've felt this process in your life? If so, write it below and share it with your group.

2. **As the fire heats the silver, the silversmith scrapes away the dross.** Webster's Dictionary defines dross as: 1. the scum that forms on the surface of molten metal 2. waste or foreign matter. God is refining you and "scraping" away the "scum" (if you will) in your life. While we at first only looked at the "scum" in our husband's lives, God is now asking us to examine our own lives. List some of the "scum" that God has brought to the surface of your life during this process.

3. **The silversmith keeps his eye on the silver to make sure the fire does not destroy it.**

First Corinthians 10:13 encourages us: *"The temptations in your life are no different from what others experience. And God is faithful. He will not allow the temptation to be more than you can stand. When you are tempted, he will show you a way out so that you can endure"* (NLT).

How do you feel knowing that God has His eyes on you personally? Briefly describe what God is seeing take place in your life through this temptation or trial.

4. **The process is complete when the silversmith sees his image clearly in the silver.**

How do you see the refining process happening in your life? How much "heat" is God allowing in your life right now, and how do you see this process transforming you more and more into God's image?

My soul melts from heaviness: strengthen me according to Your word.

PSALM 119:28, NKJV

LIFE PRINCIPLE

During the difficult and painful times, more than anything we need to hear personally from God. We cry out to God when we realize that we cannot "fix" the situations in which we find ourselves. He longs for you to invite Him into your pain. God is at work; He will not abandon you. He promises to redeem the worst messes of your life!

These trials will show that your faith is genuine. It is being tested as fire tests and purifies gold— though your faith is far more precious than gold. So when your faith remains strong through many trials, it will bring you much praise and glory and honor on the day when Jesus Christ is revealed ....

1 PETER 1:7, NLT

PRAISE IN THE STORM

[10] See, I have refined you, though not as silver; I have tested you in the furnace of affliction. [11] For my own sake, for my own sake, I do this. How can I let myself be defamed? I will not yield my glory to another.

ISAIAH 48:10-11, NIV

5. Even though God doesn't necessarily cause the difficulties in our lives, according to Isaiah 48:10 He uses them to refine us. Share in your own words how this works, and then share with the group an example of refining from your own life

As the song "Praise You in This Storm" plays, listen for answers to these questions.

- Who's being addressed in the song?

- What had the writer hoped would happen?

- Why is God praised even amidst the tears?

- From where did the help come?

Follow-up with a discussion of these questions as a group:

"And I'll praise you in this storm and I will lift my hands for You are who You are no matter where I am. And every tear I've cried You hold in your hand You never left my side. And though my heart is torn, I will praise You in this storm."²

5. How do you relate to the words of this song right now? How do you think God feels about your pain? Discuss your views as compared the song?

6. List words of encouragement that you draw from the lyrics of "Praise You in This Storm."

⁶ *So be truly glad. There is wonderful joy ahead, even though you have to endure many trials for a little while.* ⁷ *These trials will show that your faith is genuine. It is being tested as fire tests and purifies gold—though your faith is far more precious than mere gold. So when your faith remains strong through many trials, it will bring you much praise and glory and honor on the day when Jesus Christ is revealed to the whole world.*

1 PETER 1:6-7, NLT

Wow, what a promise is ours when we are faithful to God and His purposes!

A Word from Renee

"As God began His refining work in my life, I dove into the Scriptures like never before. I came across the words of Joseph in Genesis 50:20, NLT: 'You intended to harm me, but God intended it all for good. He brought me to this position so I could save the lives of many people.'

"I had heard the story of Joseph (found in Genesis 37, 39–50) my whole life. Joseph's brothers, out of jealousy, sold Joseph into slavery where he was taken to Egypt. Pharaoh quickly saw that Joseph had much to offer thus putting Joseph in high position. When the famine came, Joseph's brothers came to Egypt to get food for their father and their families. Because of Joseph's status in Pharaoh's court, he was able to save them from starving. When he finally revealed to his brothers that he was Joseph, they were afraid. Joseph assured them he would not harm them but would see that they were given what they needed. That's when Joseph said: 'You intended to harm me, but God intended it all for good. He brought me to this position so I could save the lives of many people.'

"As I read this verse, God spoke to my heart. Yes, the enemy wanted to do me harm—harm to my marriage, my husband, my family, me. HOWEVER, God had a different plan. He turned it all for good. I could see that sharing my journey with others had the potential to save many lives, marriages, and families. Yes, save them, all by His mighty right hand. I will continue to speak of His love for me and His amazing love for you."

MY PRAYER AND SUPPORT NEEDS:

MY GROUP'S PRAYER AND SUPPORT NEEDS:

Taking It Home

Questions to Take to My Heart

✳ Where am I in this refining process? Do I feel that God's presence is near or far from me right now? How ready am I really to surrender my hurts, my hopes, and my dreams to God and His plans no matter where they lead me?

Questions to Take to God

✳ God, how do you feel about me? What do you want to say to me about Your purifying fire in the midst of this difficult, painful situation?

Journal Ideas

If you have the song "Praise You in This Storm," listen to it often this week. If not, review the answers you gave to questions as you listened to the song during the session. Especially reflect on the song lyrics in the "Connecting" time; pray those words to God.

Look up Psalm 121:1-8 and write the passage on the journal page. Meditate on the precious promise God gives to you in this psalm and capture words and feelings you receive from God. Also, write down promises that you see God speaking through this psalm. Next to each promise, write a word(s) that best describes how you're feeling now.

Conclude "Taking It Home" by memorizing Philippians 4:13 in any translation you prefer. The New Living Translation states: "For I can do everything through Christ who gives me strength." My dear sisters, what a remarkable promise! Hold on to it.

My Help Comes from the Lord

ADDRESSING THE DEEPER ISSUES

GETTING STARTED - 10 MINUTES

LEADER: By now your group should be connecting well and supporting each other on the journey. Even though the group is now accustomed to deeper discussions, address this session with great sensitivity. The discussion is intended to help group members begin to address the deeper issues behind their husband's addiction and the challenges involved for them and their marriages.

NOTE: Consider placing a rose in a vase in a visible place in the room before the session.

Imagine a beautiful rose garden. Imagine the sweet aroma that penetrates the air—the vibrant, beautiful colors that steal your eyes and the tranquility that such a garden brings.

Many times we look at the surface and see the beauty but neglect to recognize the back-breaking work that went into creating the garden. Consider the commitment to:

- **Prepare the soil.** This includes tilling the ground, removing rocks and stones, and bringing in new dirt and fertilizer to create a good planting zone.

- **Select the plants and carefully place their root systems into the soil.** The gardener plans the color scheme and layout of the roses. She digs deep enough so the plants will thrive.

- **Maintain regularly.** Yes—growing beautiful roses requires watering, applying plant food, pulling weeds, pruning, and keeping them safe and healthy.

Considerable effort goes into the garden before beautiful results are evident. Thinking about the work can make you break out in a sweat and ache all over. A beautiful garden takes work—the dedicated work the gardener clearly grasps but others most likely never see.

1. Takes a moment to think of another activity that requires work to see a great payoff. When everybody has an idea, each woman should share her example with the group.

2. Are there activities in your own personal life that you could share? (Knitting, competitive sports, gardening, scrapbooking, etc.)

OPENING PRAYER

Lord, as we meet together again, fill us with Your presence. We ask that You give us Your wisdom and discernment because that's what we need. Show us that there's more to be discovered about why our husbands struggle with this issue. Give us patience, Lord. We also ask You to give us Your love for our husbands. We need You, Father. We pray and ask these things in the name of Jesus. Amen

OBJECTIVES FOR THIS SESSION

- Examine the root problems beneath pornography.

- Compare healthy sexuality to addictions.

- Discuss our vital spiritual needs.

- Embrace the "long-haul" mentality in our marriages and our lives.

DISCOVERING THE TRUTH – 35 MINUTES

> LEADER: *Before this session familiarize yourself with the Serendipity study* The Secret Seductress: Breaking the Destructive Cycle of Pornography. *In addition it would be helpful for you to scan* Shattered Vows: Hope and Healing for Women Who Have Been Sexually Betrayed *by Debra Laaser (Zondervan) and* The Seven Desires of Every Heart *by Mark and Debra Laaser (Zondervan).*

Throughout this session we will be examining passages from the book, *The Secret Seductress, Breaking the Destructive Cycle of Pornography* by Mark Laaser (used by permission). *The Secret Seductress* is the companion piece to this book, geared specifically toward our husbands. It's important that we hear from the male perspective to better understand the roots of the problem of pornography and other sex addictions.

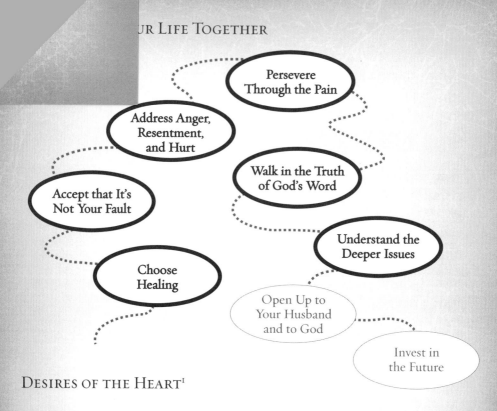

DESIRES OF THE HEART[1]

Breaking free from sex addictions would be easier if the problem just boiled down to lust, but that's far too simplistic. Just as a healthy sexual relationship is a sign of a healthy marriage, unhealthy sexual practices are a sign of more complex issues in our lives.

1. What would you say are some of the key needs and desires men generally seek to fulfill? Where do men typically search in an attempt to find satisfaction and fulfillment in life?

Many men find it difficult to identify what they think, feel, want, and need. We might ask, "Why don't you get honest about your thoughts and feelings?" The problem is that too often many of us really don't have a clue about what we really feel or want.

Social science and clinical practice point to seven core desires that men share.

Men desire to be respected and affirmed. All men want to be valued. The support and respect of others is tremendously important to a man's self-esteem. Mark Twain once said, "I can live for two months on a good compliment." Praise communicates your approval of an individual as a person.

Men desire to be included in an adventure. Each man wants to be a meaningful part of an important and noble adventure—something larger than himself.

Men desire to connect (touch in non-sexual ways). This is typically highlighted as a woman's desire, but regular physical contact through hugs, pats on the back, and the like is essential. UCLA concluded that it takes 8-10 meaningful touches a day for us to thrive.[2]

Men desire to be desired. Although taught to put on a tough exterior, if men are honest, they'll admit that they long to be passionately wanted and needed by their women.

Men desire to be a hero. Men want demonstrate that they have what it takes to deliver, to come through, to protect, defend, and rescue. Men want to leave a legacy!

Men desire to feel be grounded and secure. Security includes physical needs like shelter, food, clothing, and enough money to feel comfortable. However, it extends far beyond that into emotional, relational, and spiritual stability.

Men desire to be heard. Few men have a friend or spouse will truly listen to what they have to say. A listening ear speaks volumes about our value to another person.

2. Which "desire" do you feel your husband would view as being most fulfilled?
   In which one would your husband feel the least fulfilled?

3. As you consider the desires of a man's heart, are there areas where you could be more encouraging to your husband or could more effectively reinforce the needs he has?

WALKING WOUNDED

Ideally, all seven desires of the heart would be fulfilled during childhood. While nobody has perfect parents or a life without pain, some men grow up with few of these needs met well. Instead of being cared for, they are deeply wounded. They may ultimately feel abandoned, isolated, and disillusioned.

We all experience pain at times and there are many ways to "numb out" or escape that pain. Our enemy strategically shoots arrows of pain and loss. He uses the wounds in our lives to distort our perception of who we are. He then continually whispers lies about who we are, who God is, God's heart toward us, and the intimacy God wants us to share with Him.

Jesus and Paul explained what goes on in our hearts as wrestle with our distorted beliefs:

[Jesus said:] [20] It is what comes from inside that defiles you. [21] For from within, out of a person's heart, come evil thoughts, sexual immorality, theft, murder, [22] adultery, greed, wickedness, deceit, lustful desires, envy, slander, pride, and foolishness. [23] All these vile things come from within; they are what defile you.

MARK 7:20-23, NLT

[Paul added:] [15] For I do not understand what I am doing, because I do not practice what I want to do, but I do what I hate. [16] And if I do what I do not want to do, I agree with the law that it is good. [17] So now I am no longer the one doing it, but it is the sin living in me.

ROMANS 7:15-17, HCSB

4. According to Jesus in Mark 7:20-23, where do the lies, false agreements, and vows become embedded? What impact can these deeply rooted false beliefs have in our lives?

5. What's the inner struggle Paul describes in Romans 7:15-17? What does Paul imply about his identity, the truest thing about himself? What does he conclude is doing these destructive things?[3]

FALSE INTIMACY

In research of 1,000 sex addicts, Pat Carnes found 97% were emotionally abused, 74% physically abused, and 81% sexually abused. When we carry wounds of the past, we search desperately for something—anything—to fill our empty places. We become easy prey for counterfeits that promise to fulfill our desires. For example, masturbation, in addition to a hormonal experience, can be a way of self-gratification and self-medicating. On the surface, porn and unhealthy sexual behaviors seem to meet our desires. Let's see how God feels:

[22] Although they claimed to be wise, they became fools [23] and exchanged the glory of the immortal God for images made to look like mortal men and birds and animals and reptiles. [24] Therefore God gave them over in the sinful desires of their hearts to sexual impurity for the degrading of their bodies with one another. [25] They exchanged the truth of God for a lie, and worshipped and served created things rather than the Creator—who is forever praised. [28] ... He gave them over to a depraved mind, to do what ought not to be done. [29] They have become filled with every kind of wickedness, evil, greed and depravity.

ROMANS 1:22-25, 28-29, NIV

6. Why is it that people so easily abandon God in exchange for counterfeit lovers or addictions? Has there been a time when you left God in exchange for counterfeit happiness? If you're comfortable, share an example with the group.

7. How does God feel when people seek to fulfill their deepest longings with substitutes rather that wrestling through barriers to intimacy with Him? Why do you think your husband settles for substitutes?[4]

PRINCIPLE FOR LIVING

All the false substitutes the world offers can never satisfy us the way genuine intimacy with God can. To find healing, men addicted to porn and other sexual activities must begin to acknowledge that all their strivings to satisfy their thirsts are extreme failures.

8. Will you commit to pray for your husband and his "deeper issues"? Can you commit to do this in a way that's not nagging or intrusive but centered in love and respect?

9. What part of this problem do you view as your husband's? What part do you see yourself playing in this struggle?

EMBRACING THE TRUTH – 20 MINUTES

As we embrace the truth we will continue to examine excerpts from *The Secret Seductress*. Ask God to keep your heart open to the truth as we look at research findings and offer support for men who are struggling. It's easy to get closed off because we don't understand. Ask God to show you something new that will help you respond more effectively to your husband's struggle.

Healthy Sex and Destructive Sex

Our culture and the Christian church are experiencing a great deal of turmoil in the area of sexuality. There are essentially two primary areas of struggle:

1. **Inhibited sexual desire**—God's desire for a person's sexual life remains elusive and hurtful.

2. **Sexual compulsion**—Forceful, difficult-to-control urges drive a person into a secret life of shame and self-hatred because he can't even live out his own values. This is the realm of the sex addict.

1. In your view, what's the difference between healthy sexuality and sex addiction? What do you see as the healing goal for someone with a destructive or unhealthy sexual problem?

2. In your personal opinion, what's the purpose(s) of sex?

Behavior & Thoughts	Sex Addict	Non-Sex Addict
Thinks about sex	Constantly	Periodically
Encounters sexual stimuli, such as pornography or an attractive person	Initiates a cycle of sexual thoughts and hoped-for sex activities. Disregards moral/spiritual boundaries.	Acknowledges the stimulus and may even be aroused, but considers and regards all moral and spiritual boundaries.
Masturbation	Becomes a habitual pattern used to medicate feelings.	Does not allow it to become a pattern or source of comfort.
Experience of sexual sin	Battles the cycle of guilt and shame but repeats the sin.	Confesses, turns away from, and learns from the experience.
Marital sexuality	Selfish use of spouse to meet needs and avoid feelings and intimacy.	Fulfillment in meeting needs of spouse too. Experiences deep emotional and spiritual intimacy.

3. What key insight or new perspective from this chart stands out to you? [5]

PRINCIPLE FOR LIVING

Healing from sexual addictions is not as simple as just pulling a plug and everything is fixed. Sex addictions are one expression of deeper emotional and spiritual issues. If the deeper issues are not addressed, sooner or later the plug will be reconnected.

4. What were your initial expectations for your husband's healing from porn or other sex issues? How should we as wives respond to our husbands now that we understand there's no overnight fix to his struggle?

A WORD FROM RENEE

"Clay and I had finished writing our book I Surrender All: Rebuilding a Marriage Broken by Pornography. Because of the book we were invited to our first Christian Booksellers Convention. I was nervous because I knew the book was honest. After all it has the "P" word right on the cover. What would people think? Would they embrace us or avoid us like the plague?

"After our book signing, we were whisked away for interviews. My head was spinning! My face physically hurt from smiling and talking so much yet I was thankful for the positive response to the book. As we walked into one of our last interviews, there was a woman waiting for us. As we entered, she asked: 'Is this the pornographer?' I couldn't believe that's how she addressed my husband. She didn't care for our book and proceeded to ask Clay when God had healed him. Clay told her that God had forgiven him but he was not completely healed from his struggle. She challenged him, indicating that she could rub some holy oil on his head and heal him right there on the spot. We didn't quite know how to take her. Yes, I believe that God could 100 percent heal my husband and deliver him from this struggle if He wanted to take that route. Clay just calmly thanked her and quoted: 'God blesses those who patiently endure testing and temptation. Afterward they will receive the crown of life that God has promised to those who love him' (James 1:12, NLT). I was glad the day was over and glad to be by Clay's side."

5. What could happen when a guy identifies himself as the sum of his addictions or failures?

6. How can we view our husbands as *more* than "the pornographer"? How can we remind encourage and our husbands that they are *not* their sins any more than we are our sins.

CONNECTING – 20 MINUTES

> *LEADER: Continue to help group members deepen their connections with God and with their own hearts. Don't be hesitant to share your struggles so others will feel safer in sharing. Group members may need more encouragement now than at any other point along the way so far.*

> *LEADER INSTRUCTIONS FOR THE GROUP EXPERIENCE: Have a CD/MP3 player queued up to play the song "In Better Hands" by Natalie Grant. The song is on her CD entitled* Relentless *or available for download from your favorite music site on the Web. Lead the group in a discussion using the questions that follow as a guide.*

The first few lines from the song "In Better Hands" by Natalie Grant read:

"It's hard to stand on shifting sand. It's hard to shine in the shadows of the night.
You can't be free if you don't reach for help, and you can't love if you don't love yourself.
But there is hope when my faith runs out ... cuz I'm in better hands now."[6]

1. Do you feel as if you're trying to "stand on shifting sand?" What is it that gives you the most trouble with your equilibrium?

2. As a group listen closely to the lyrics of the song "In Better Hands." In the space below record the emotions that sweep across your emotional radar as you listen to the words.

Share with the group the emotions that the song brought out as you listened.

3. Consider what things can sometimes keep you from releasing your fears into God's hands. If this is a struggle for you, what do you think is really going on inside?

4. Can you honestly say: "I am strong all because of You?" Why or why not?

Think back to "Getting Started" discussion. Just like a garden, your marriage needs hands that will work diligently and daily. Let's ask God to be those Hands. God will not leave you alone. He's your loving Papa; He will see you through.

Read aloud Psalm 121:7-8, NLT: "The LORD keeps you from all harm and watches over your life. The LORD keeps watch over you as you come and go, both now and forever."

MY PRAYER AND SUPPORT NEEDS:

MY GROUP'S PRAYER AND SUPPORT NEEDS:

LEADER: *After the women have shared their prayer needs, pray aloud for each one of them and their voiced needs. Hearing someone pray specifically for you is encouraging.*

Taking It Home

A Question to Take to My Heart

❋ Am I willing to be the support and encouragement my husband needs throughout this struggle? What, if any, resentment am I still carrying that's holding me back from fully reengaging with my husband.

A Question to Take to God

❋ God, we reviewed the seven desires of a man's heart this week. Which of these does my husband really need help with right now? What could I do that would be most beneficial in his healing journey?

Journal Ideas

Spend time alone with God. Ask Him to guide you as you seek to support your husband and see total healing in his life. Most men will be resistant to explore their past hurts so pray for a softening of your husband's heart and good opportunities for discussions (even if brief). You cannot force the exploration process on him, but in order for full healing to take place, he must be willing to uncover the root causes that led him to this behavior. Write in your journal the desires you have for your husband and his deeper issues. Recall the garden illustration. List the "thorns" that you are up against, as well as the beautiful things—the "roses" that God has given you in your life.

Also, ask yourself if you're really willing to do the work it will take to see God do something beautiful in your life, in your husband's life, and in your marriage. Be honest. If you don't feel like going on, ask God again for the strength you need to continue the journey.

ROOTS, THORNS, AND ROSES

_____

_____

_____

_____

_____

_____

_____

_____

_____

_____

_____

_____

_____

_____

_____

_____

_____

_____

_____

_____

_____

_____

NOTES:

1. Mark R. Laaser, Michael Christian. *The Secret Seductress: Breaking the Destructive Cycle of Pornography* (Nashville: Serendipity by LifeWay, 2007), 81-82.

2. "Helping engaged couples find A.W.E. in their upcoming marriage," Jim Burns, Pastors.com [cited 19 January 2007]. Available on the Internet: http://www.pastors.com/article.asp?ArtID=9716.

3. Laaser, 81-82.   4. Ibid., 85-86.   5. Ibid., 22-23.

6. "In Better Hands." Words and music by Catt Gravitt, Jim Daddario, and Thom Hardwell. © Copyright 2006 Two Girls and a Pen/Jim Daddario Music/Thom Hardwell Music. All rights reserved.

My End of the Bargain

Getting Started - 10 minutes

> LEADER: *Even though the focus of "Getting Started" is to help you recognize how difficult it can be to stick with a commitment, the questions will allow for lighthearted answers and group laughter.*

Have you ever been swayed by a late-night infomercial? Even though it was costly, you ordered the latest and greatest exercise machine that promised to slim you down in just minutes a day! You even assured your husband that you'd use it every day. Once it arrived you spent just enough time on it to determine that it was way too difficult to use. That miracle machine became merely a "hook" on which to hang your clothes.

1. Can you think of a time when you were initially gung ho about an item or activity only to fizzle out? Share your experience with the group.

2. How many times do you suppose you've repeated this pattern? You may or may not want to share your answer with the group (ha).

Opening Prayer

God, when we stop to think about it, we're astounded that You love us so deeply and passionately. We want to live our lives in a way that honors You. You know the road ahead of us will be difficult at times, but Father, You also see the great moments too. Almighty God, we want Your blessing on our marriages; make them better than they've ever been. We love You. See us through. Amen

Objectives for this Session

- Examine my part in rebuilding of our marriage relationship.

- Discuss pitfalls to avoid in the rebuilding process.

- Embrace this current challenge as an experience designed to make me more like Christ.

DISCOVERING THE TRUTH – 30 MINUTES

RECLAIMING YOUR LIFE TOGETHER

Although it helps to have some understanding the deeper issues with which our husbands struggle, we still find it challenging to open up to our husbands and to God after what's occurred. In today's session we will look at some ways we can be more open.

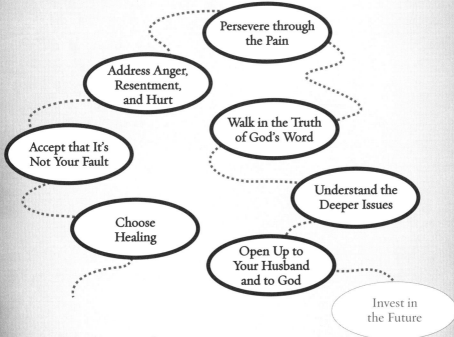

Persevere through the Pain

Address Anger, Resentment, and Hurt

Accept that It's Not Your Fault

Walk in the Truth of God's Word

Understand the Deeper Issues

Choose Healing

Open Up to Your Husband and to God

Invest in the Future

WHAT IS MY PART IN REBUILDING?

That's a tough question because you may be thinking: *My part? Am I still a part of the same support group that's been helping me deal with the pain? What do you mean my part in rebuilding?!*

Well yes, you're still in the same room, with the same people, working through the same healing journey, but it's important to examine your part in rebuilding.

1. What's your definition of rebuilding in a relationship?

2. Do you think it's fair that you're being asked to contribute to the rebuilding process? (This wasn't exactly your sin.) Be honest in your response and explain your thinking.

A Word from Renee

"After Clay's confession I invested time in securing resources that would help me through that tough time. I stumbled upon the book The Power of a Praying Wife by Stormie Omartian. As I read this powerful little book, God began to change my perspective on my situation. Even as I write this, it seems like it was just yesterday when God turned the light bulb on in my mind and heart. I was looking for something that was going to help me. To my amazement God was steering me toward something that would benefit Clay. Then I began to realize this truth: **Praying for my husband absolutely had the power to change his life and consequently mine.** I also began to realize if it did not change him on my time table, God would give the strength to not only get through, but to thrive. Why? Simply because of my obedience to His Word in aligning my heart with God's, I would be changed! My heart, my perspective, and my life would be changed. My ongoing encounters with God also would impact my husband, my children, my family, and my friends."

3. In the midst of hurt and a flood of negative emotions, what schemes could the Enemy use to turn us away from the power of committed praying for our husbands? How can the group encourage and support a life-changing habit of prayer?

Let's look at a prayer from *Power of a Praying Wife*. You may find that when you cannot muster the words to pray this prayer will likely express the words you need to say to God.

A Prayer for Integrity [1]

"Lord, I pray that you would make my husband a man of integrity, according to Your standards. Give him strength to say 'Yes' when he should say 'Yes,' and courage to say 'No' when he should say 'No.' Enable him to stand for what he knows is right and not waver under pressure from the world. Don't let him be a man who is 'always learning and never able to come to a knowledge of the truth' (2 Timothy 3:7). Give him, instead a teachable spirit that is willing to listen to the voice of wisdom and grow in Your ways.

"Make him a man who lives by truth. Help him to walk with Your Spirit of truth at all times (John 16:13). Be with him to bear witness to the truth so that in times of pressure he will act on it with confidence (1 John 1:8-9). Where he has erred in this and other matters, give him a heart that is quick to confess his mistakes. For You have said in Your Word, 'If we say that we have no sin, we deceive ourselves, and the truth is not in us. If we confess our sins, He is faithful and just to forgive us our sins and cleanse us from all unrighteousness' (1 John 1:8-9). Don't let him be deceived. Don't let him live a lie in any way. Bind mercy and truth around his neck and write them on the tablet of his heart so he will find favor and high esteem in the sight of God and man" (Proverbs 3:3-4; NIV)."

4. Has there been a time in your life when you prayed such a pointed and intense prayer for your husband? For yourself? If so, share your experience to encourage the group.

5. How do you feel about praying Scripture over your husband's life as well as over your own? How might applying Scripture to your prayer life take it to a different level?

As you become more aware of praying Scripture, verses will jump off the page when you're reading the Bible. You'll find yourself praying those Scriptures for yourself and your loved ones. You'll see God honor His words to work in and through your life.

¹³ Are you hurting? Pray. Do you feel great? Sing. ¹⁴ Are you sick? Call the church leaders together to pray and anoint you with oil in the name of the Master. ¹⁵ Believing-prayer will heal you, and Jesus will put you on your feet. And if you've sinned, you'll be forgiven—healed inside and out. ¹⁶ Make this your common practice: Confess your sins to each other and pray for each other so that you can live together whole and healed. The prayer of a person living right with God is something powerful.

JAMES 5:13-16, THE MESSAGE

6. According to James 5:13-16, what's the role of prayer? God's formula in James 5:16 for living well together runs counter to our desire to hide what's really going on. How would it feel to have this kind of relationship with your friends? Your husband?

LIFE PRINCIPLE

Most of us really don't believe that prayer has any effect; if we did, we'd pray more. But the Bible's key answer to all the hardest stuff in life is to build up one another in community ... and to pray, pray, pray. Take it all to your Father!

THE BEST COUNSELOR

We truly need counsel from godly people, but we must be careful to seek God's counsel first and foremost. In Isaiah 9:6, Jesus is named "Wonderful Counselor, Mighty God, Eternal Father, Prince of Peace" (HCSB). See anything in Isaiah 9:6 you need?

7. Take a moment to consider what you most need from this list of descriptors. Share your answer with the group and tell why you chose it.

¹⁰ [God's] Spirit searches out everything and shows us God's deep secrets. ... ¹² And we have received God's Spirit (not the world's spirit), so we can know the wonderful things God has freely given us. ¹³ When we tell you these things, we do not use words that come from human wisdom. Instead, we speak words given to us by the Spirit, using the Spirit's words to explain spiritual truths. ¹⁴ But people who aren't spiritual can't receive these truths from God's Spirit. It all sounds foolish to them and they can't understand it, for only those who are spiritual can understand what the Spirit means.

1 CORINTHIANS 2:10-14, NLT

⁴ Take delight in the LORD, and he will give you your heart's desires. ⁵ Commit everything you do to the LORD. Trust him, and he will help you.

PSALM 37:4-5, NLT

8. As you read 1 Corinthians 2:10-12 and Psalm 37:4-5, how vital is listening in our prayer times with God? What have been some situations in the past when God clearly spoke to you or directed you as you went to Him, waited, and listened?

EMBRACING THE TRUTH – 35 MINUTES

LEADER: Focus on helping group members recognize the challenge they will face as they seek healing and restoration. Group members should be able to take some "handles" with them from this section that will prove invaluable in the healing process. Invite volunteers to read Scriptures.

THE RAGING BATTLE

Get ready! Satan won't be happy about your turning to Almighty God for power and wisdom. He'll loathe your fervent prayers for your husband and your marriage. The enemy attacks may even intensify. Often he shows up just when God is preparing to do something great in our lives. Until Jesus finally establishes His eternal kingdom, the fierce battle between God and the forces of evil rages in the heavens and spills over to earth. Daniel knew well the strength of the enemy, but he also knew the vastly superior power of God.

[18] *Listen, my God, and hear. Open Your eyes and see our desolations and the city called by Your name. For we are not presenting our petitions before You based on our righteous acts, but based on Your abundant compassion.* [19] *Lord, hear! Lord, forgive! Lord, listen and act! My God, for Your own sake, do not delay, because Your city and Your people are called by Your name.* [20] *While I was speaking, praying, confessing my sin and the sin of my people Israel, and presenting my petition before Yahweh my God ...* [21] *Gabriel [came] ...* [22] *and gave me this explanation: "Daniel, I've come now to give you understanding. ...* [23] *for you are treasured by God.*

DANIEL 9:18-23, HCSB

1. What's the tone and attitude of Daniel's prayer in Daniel 9? What can we learn from this prayer about going to battle for our husbands, marriages, families, and friends?

2. The answer to Daniel's desperate pleas didn't come right away, but Daniel didn't give up or give in. How and why did God respond?

⁶ [God] gives us even more grace to stand against such evil desires. As the Scriptures say, "God opposes the proud but favors the humble." ⁷ So humble yourselves before God. Resist the devil, and he will flee from you.

JAMES 4:6-7, NLT

3. What divinely powerful resources are highlighted in James 4:6-7 for battling the forces of evil? What are some other divinely powerful weapons that you've used or studied?

A WORD FROM RENEE

"I remember a time when Clay was really depressed. He was trying to deal with the issues from his past that had brought him to his struggle with porn. He was seeing our pastor as well as another counselor. A dark cloud seemed to be hanging over Clay. Soon the dark cloud was hovering over our home. I was trying to be supportive. Oh how I was praying that Clay's depression wouldn't perpetuate his "slipping up" and turning to porn again! I was gripped by fear.

"I remember having a dream. I saw Satan sitting on the fence in our backyard. I woke up to find that Clay had left our room and was trying to sleep on the couch. He was in a really dark place to the point he was he was really beating himself up, saying things that the Enemy was putting into his mind. I told him about my dream and commented: 'Satan may be out there on the fence, but he can't touch this house or us!' I opened my Bible and started reading from Proverbs and inserting Clay's name in the Scripture. Needless to say, this battle left me exhausted but confident of two things. One, we are in a real spiritual battle for our marriages, and two, at the name of Jesus, Satan flees!"

Dressing for Success

Hopefully, you've seen and understand more clearly the depths of the fierce battle we're up against. Gone are the simple, nice prayers of polite Christianity. Gone are the short, pat answers to problems. We are engaged in a battle. Are you prepared? Do you know what it looks like to put on "the Armor of God"? **Girls, it's time to "dress for success"!**

[10] Be strengthened by the Lord and by His vast strength. [11] Put on the full armor of God so that you can stand against the tactics of the Devil. [12] For our battle is not against flesh and blood, but against the rulers, against the authorities, against the world powers of this darkness, against the spiritual forces of evil in the heavens. [13] This is why you must take up the full armor of God, so that you may be able to resist in the evil day, and having prepared everything, to take your stand. [14] Stand, therefore, with <u>truth</u> like a belt around your waist, <u>righteousness</u> like armor on your chest, [15] and your feet sandaled with <u>readiness for the gospel of peace</u>. [16] In every situation take the shield of <u>faith</u>, and with it you will be able to extinguish the flaming arrows of the evil one. [17] Take the helmet of <u>salvation</u>, and the sword of the Spirit, which is <u>God's word</u>. [18] With every prayer and request, <u>pray at all times</u> in the Spirit, and stay alert in this, with all perseverance and intercession for all the saints.
Ephesians 6:10-18, hcsb, emphasis added

Belt of Truth: The waist or abdomen was generally believed to be the seat of emotions. To protect this area with truth is to commit your emotions to believe the truth.

4. How can we learn to trust even when doubt tries to overwhelm us?

Armor of Righteousness: Our hearts must be kept pure and righteous so pain doesn't lead us to temptation. Sin gives a foothold to the Enemy.

5. How can we avoid retaliation or bitterness toward our husbands?

Ready Shoes: We should be about our Father's business: spreading the gospel of peace and reconciliation. An undaunted sense of this mission keeps us headed in the right direction.

6. How can we contribute to the reconciliation process in our homes?

Shield of Faith: The Evil One is "the accuser" and "the father of liars." He launches his fiery darts to instill doubt, fear, and guilt. Faith acts as an invisible shield that deflects false accusations/lies about God, us, and others (such as our husbands).

7. Where can we find the courage and strength to continue in the heat of the battle?

Helmet of Salvation: A helmet protects the head, that is, our thoughts. Assurance of salvation and God's presence is a mighty defense against doubt, insecurity, and false beliefs.

8. How can I be sure that God can and will heal our hurts? Redeem our lives?

Sword: The words of God, the only offensive weapon in this armor, were used by the Lord Jesus against Satan. The living word is powerful, effective, and instructive.

9. What will help me wield my sword more effectively?

Constant Prayer: God counts it a privilege to come alongside us in our battles. We must keep in constant communication with the Holy Spirit for direction, encouragement, and divine power. Our prayers for one another are vital, carrying greater power than we know.

10. How can we make prayer a priority?

BONUS DISCUSSION: PRACTICAL STEPS FOR THE CHILDREN

We have listed some practical steps we as parents put in place to help us as we maneuvered through Clay's public confession and the our recovery. They may be helpful to you too. (NOTE: To save time, read this section at home)

Get a sitter.
We asked friends and family to baby-sit the girls to give us time alone to talk. We always took the girls to the sitter's house and returned to our home where we could talk privately. Trust me, you don't want to have a meltdown and start crying in the mall food court.

Show affection to one another.
We felt it was extremely important to show affection toward one another around our children. I'm not talking about make-out sessions, rather holding hands, giving a kiss, or just sitting beside each other on the sofa. These are huge steps especially when there's tension, but it shows your commitment to each other. Your kids will definitely notice.

Show respect.

Respect is vital in every relationship, and most certainly in marriage and parent-child relationships. I could be angry with Clay, but I still knew I needed to show him respect. I was aware that the girls were watching the way I treated their dad. We know that what's watched is caught. We didn't want them to have respect issues as they grew up.

Consider counseling.

We were open about our need to see someone who could help us make our marriage better and stronger. We wanted our children to see it as a sign of strength, not weakness. If your children are older, you may want to consider godly professional counsel for them.

Point them to God.

It's important to continually and gently fold God into your husband's life and the lives of your children. Be faithful in church fellowship, Bible reading, and sharing Bible truths with your children. Let your children see you pray, and pray with them. You may receive a few eye-rolls, especially from teenagers, but they'll come to realize that their mom cares deeply about her walk with God and her family's. What a lesson to teach even in difficult times!

Be an example.

You've probably heard: "More is caught than taught." Whether or not our husbands are fully on board with us, we're responsible to God for our response and the example we live out in front of our children. Without healing in our marriage, our children will be exposed to bitterness, arguments, and a lack of respect that they could carry into marriage one day. Do we close down or try to hide, or do we run to God and live?

⁹ For I the LORD your God, am a jealous God who will not tolerate your affection for any other gods. I lay the sins of the parents upon their children; the entire family is affected—even children in the third and fourth generations of those who reject me. ¹⁰ But I lavish unfailing love for a thousand generations on those who love me and obey my commands.

DEUTERONOMY 5:9-10, NLT

11. Deuteronomy 5:9-10 contrasts God's judgment and mercy. How serious are the sin's consequences? What can be expected by those who turn back to love and obey God?

12. Do you see the vital importance of supporting your husband and remaining dependent on God's guidance as you move forward? Will you ask God to help you stay faithful to Him and to show your children a mom who loves God and is faithful to His commands?

Narrow or Wide?

Matthew 7:13 says, "You can enter God's Kingdom only through the narrow gate. The highway to hell is broad, and its gate is wide for the man who chooses that way" (NLT). We remind our children (and ourselves) that they *will* be confronted with difficult choices. Decisions will be tough. We have a simple saying in the Crosse house. We encourage our kids to ask themselves: **"Narrow or Wide?"**

CONNECTING – 10 MINUTES

LEADER: Use "Connecting" to help group members deepen their connection with God and with one another. Continue to encourage the women taking this 'narrow" road to healing with you.

It's been said: "Every one of us is either headed on our way into a trial, in the middle of a trial, or just coming out of a trial." Thankfully, God is always at work redeeming and restoring. He offers us incredible hope if we'll persevere through the pain of life!

¹ The Spirit of the Sovereign LORD is on me, because the LORD has anointed me to preach good news to the poor. He has sent me to bind up the brokenhearted, to proclaim freedom to the captives and release from darkness for the prisoners, ² to proclaim the year of the LORD's and the day of vengeance of our God to comfort all who mourn, ³ and provide for those who grieve in Zion—to bestow on them a crown of beauty instead of ashes, the oil of gladness instead of mourning, and a garment of praise instead of a spirit of despair. They will be called oaks of righteousness, a planting of the LORD for the day of his splendor.

ISAIAH 61:1-3, NIV

1. Only God can bring beauty from ashes. We must be willing to ask ourselves: Can I let the ashes of the past rise up to something beautiful? What, if anything, is preventing this?

2. What rays of hope does God offer in Isaiah 61:1-3? For which ray do you most need prayer right now?

MY PRAYER AND SUPPORT NEEDS:

MY GROUP'S PRAYER AND SUPPORT NEEDS:

Stand together and lock arms or hold hands with the others in your group. Offer specific prayers for each woman and her situation. Ask God to bind her up, set her free, comfort her, fill her with gladness and praise, and replace the ashes of her life with a crown of beauty.

TAKING IT HOME

JOURNAL AND SHARING EXERCISE

This week, focus on journaling your thoughts and desires at this point in the rebuilding process. Include two versions as you write—one focused toward God and the other toward your husband.

Version One: This version will serve as a "pouring out moment" between you and God. Tell Him all your hurts, your desires for your husband's deliverance, and your dreams for your spiritual growth and legacy.

Version Two: In this version, write a "shorter" one for your husband to read. Be careful in this. Ask God to help you proceed in love and not criticism or sarcasm. With God's help you can write in a way that will bring honor and respect to both God and to your husband. Share with your husband your hurt, but quickly get to your hope in God to do a mighty work in your marriage and your home.

NOTE: Before sharing what you have written, spend time praying that God will provide the right moment to share this with your husband. You'll be amazed at what God can do if you ask. God can soften the most hardened heart and bring about amazing results when we ask and wait expectantly!

OPENING UP ...

_____

_____

_____

_____

_____

_____

_____

_____

_____

_____

_____

_____

_____

_____

_____

_____

_____

_____

_____

_____

_____

_____

Consider memorizing Job 23:10-11, HCSB:

Yet He knows the way I have taken; when He has tested me, I will emerge as pure gold. My feet have followed in His tracks; I have kept to His way and not turned aside.

What a testimony to the world and a legacy to leave for your children!

NOTES:

1. Stormie Omartian. _The Power of a Praying Wife_ (Eugene, OR: Harvest House Publishers, 1997).

HOW CAN I MAKE THIS WORK?

GETTING STARTED - 15 MINUTES

LEADER: Since this is the final session of Reclaiming Stolen Intimacy, you may want to allow more time for personal sharing than in previous sessions. This study may have served as a lifeline to the women. They've received "tools" to use as they journey on. Now the real challenges begin.

LEADER INSTRUCTIONS FOR THE GROUP EXPERIENCE: Provide a 3x5-inch note card and pen for each group member.

In this session we'll discuss how to continue in the process of healing and reclaiming intimacy as we strive to build a marriage and a live a life that will leave a lasting and godly legacy. But before we move into the heavy stuff, let's see how well we have gotten to know our fellow group members in the past seven weeks.

On a 3x5-inch note card fill in the information asked for below. Then fold the card in half and place it in a basket. One by one draw the cards from the basket. As the descriptors are read aloud, the group will guess which women matches each card.

1. The last book I read.

2. The latest song I downloaded or CD that I bought.

3. My friends and family say that I am famous for _____.

4. One word to describe me is _____.

5. People might be surprised to know _____ about me.

OPENING PRAYER

Lord, as we meet together here for the last session in this study, we thank you for showing us Your presence in our lives. While there will no doubt be difficult days ahead, we know that You are at work and will never abandon us. We need Your continued presence at work in our homes, in our lives, and the lives of our husbands. Give us strength as we press on to rebuild our lives and our marriages. Amen.

Objectives for this Session

- Discuss the importance of taking care of yourself.

- Invest in your healing as well as your husband's.

- Prepare your heart to handle setbacks.

- Learn how to invest in your marriage.

Discovering the Truth – 35 Minutes

LEADER: *"Discovering the Truth" will mainly center on how the women can invest in the future. Be sure to leave ample time for "Embracing the Truth" and the final "Connecting" wrap-up.*

Reclaiming Your Life Together

This is our last session in *Reclaiming Stolen Intimacy*. However, in reality the journey is really just beginning. Now is the time to invest in the future if you want to see healing and restoration in your life and the lives of those around you.

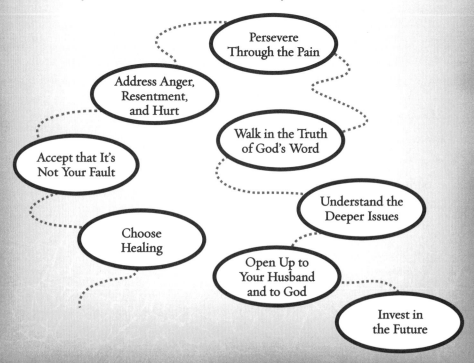

How you choose to embrace God and His truth will determine the outcome of the rest of your journey. We want you to hear again that God loves you and He wants His best for your life. As you continue to love, heal, and grow spiritually, spend extra time taking care of yourself. The goal is for you to be whole—physically, emotionally, relationally, and spiritually.

INVESTING IN MY HEALTH

1. As a wife, mother, employee, and home manager, you're always taking care of others. How well are you doing at taking care of yourself? Are you willing to invest time to take care of myself? (Discuss the responses.)

LIFE PRINCIPLE
The Bible and medical science teach that our spiritual health, emotional health, and physical health are all integrally linked. Healthy living and self-control can glorify God and make you more effective in your daily walk with Him and in your relationships with others. We can be fit without becoming obsessive and narcissistic.

A WORD FROM RENEE

"Believe it or not I've become a crossword puzzle junkie. I look forward to opening the morning paper and jumping right into my first answer. I get so immersed, I even let my cereal get soggy. It sounds silly—call me a nerd—but this is something I do for me. Some other "me things" I do to relax incude photography, listening to music, gardening, and bike riding.

"We all need something we do that's just for us. It helps us be better moms, wives, friends, and daughters of the King."

2. Name something that is exclusively yours—something you do for your enjoyment. If you can't think of one, it's time to get one. What have you thought you might enjoy?

3. Spend some time in the group discussing suggestions or ideas for maintaining your physical, emotional, and spiritual well-being. (Remember, taking care of yourself is not selfish; it's essential. You won't be able to care for others if you don't care for yourself.)

As a group, listen to a song that is one of my personal favorites: "Jesus I am Resting, Resting." I encourage you to listen often to this song. You may want to get a copy of the CD, or you can listen to it at http://www.cyberhymnal.org/htm/j/i/jiamrest.htm.

LEADER INSTRUCTIONS FOR THE GROUP EXPERIENCE: Have a CD player queued up to play the song, "Jesus I Am Resting, Resting" from the CD Awakening, Vol. 1, presented by Christ Community Church. After playing the song, read aloud the four lines of the song below. Engage the women in discussing the questions that follow.

Ladies, every word of this song is for us. However, for a moment let's focus on these lyrics:

"Thou hast bid me gaze upon Thee, and Thy beauty fills my soul, for, by Thy transforming power, Thou hast made me whole."

4. What is Jesus inviting us to do? What do you think happens when we can keep our focus on Him despite our circumstances?

5. Think of a verse or chorus from one of your favorite songs—one that speaks peace or encouragement into your life. Share your favorite with the group.

6. It sounds trite, but it's a critical question for healing to occur: Do you really want to be well and "whole?" What can make you whole?

Investing in My Husband's Healing

Let's look at the needs a husband has from his wife and how we can striv[e]
needs. These needs come from research findings of William Harley in th[e]
Her Needs. Our husbands are far from perfect, and so are we! God passionately loves us in
all our messiness, and that's the kind of love He longs to see in our homes.

A husband needs to have the respect of his wife.
He needs her sincere admiration. "Each man must love his wife as he loves himself, and
the wife must respect her husband" (Ephesians 5:33, NLT). Will you pray and ask God to
help you express respect for your husband?

A husband needs appreciation.
A wife needs to express gratitude for her husband's life, faithfulness, work, provision,
and care. Think of one example of something you can be grateful for that your husband
has done for you. Share that with him. (Don't let this be just a one-time thing. Look for
examples on a regular basis to show appreciation.)

A husband also needs affirmation.
A wife should speak kind words and assure her husband of her love and fidelity. "She
opens her mouth in wisdom, and the teaching of kindness is on her tongue" (Proverbs
31:26, NASB). Ask God to help "season" your words with kindness. Most of us have room
for improvement in this area. How often do you speak with anger? With kindness?

A husband needs a wife he can trust.
"Her husband trusts her without reserve, and never has reason to regret it. Never spiteful,
she treats him generously all her life long." (Proverbs 31:11-12, The Message). Are you
trustworthy? Do you think your husband could say this verse about you?

A husband needs sexual fulfillment and sensitivity on the part of his wife to this need.
"The husband should fulfill his wife's sexual needs, and the wife should fulfill her
husband's needs. The wife gives authority over her body to her husband, and the husband
gives authority over his body to his wife" (1 Corinthians 7:3-4, NLT). Would you be
willing to pray and ask God to help you become a better lover to your husband? Stay
open here. This is not a negative statement to discourage you because if we're truthful,
we know there's room for improvement.

A husband needs a home to which he can go for comfort and peace.
"And Isaac brought Rebekah into his mother Sarah's tent, and she became his wife. He
loved her deeply, and she was a special comfort to him after the death of his mother"
(Genesis 24:67, NLT). Is your home a place where your family can go to experience
peace and comfort? A shelter from the world?

A Side Note from Renee

I discovered a wonderful book that has become such an amazing resource to me that I want to share with you. The title is Intimate Issues by Linda Dillow and Lorraine Pintus. The book really opened my eyes to God's design for sex within marriage. It's very open and honest and, most importantly, biblically sound. I actually led a book study and hosted a conference with the authors a few years ago. A lot of us are carrying unhealthy sexual baggage and need to hear God's truth. Read the book; you won't regret it.

Linda and Lorraine also contributed to a creative resource called Simply Romantic Nights with Dennis and Barbara Rainey of FamilyLife. It's filled with wonderful, tasteful but to-the-point games and ideas to add more romance and intimacy in your marriage. The kit includes cards you can place in your husband's car or briefcase with suggestions for intimate times. Intimacy with your husband should not be an obligation but a joy. Truly it can be!

A husband needs to find his wife attractive and be proud of her.
He needs to share mutual fellowship and fun with her. "Her children stand and bless her. Her husband praises her. There are many virtuous and capable women in the world, but you surpass them all!" (Proverbs 31:28-29 NLT). Will you commit to pray that God raises you up to be a woman of whom this could be said?

LIFE PRINCIPLE
Your imperfect husband should be considered a precious gift from God, to be treated with sensitivity, tenderness, love, and respect. To meet his needs requires time: time to listen; time to touch; time to do kind deeds; and time to be creative in acts of love.

8. How can we do a better job of treating our husbands with respect? Showing appreciation? Sensitively providing for their sexual fulfillment? Making home a safe place for them? Asking ourselves attractive? Brainstorm ideas with your group.

A WORD FROM RENEE

"Clay and I built a new house after he confessed to his struggle with porn. I was excited to live in a new house that was porn-free. I found comfort in knowing that there had been no porn within its "clean" walls.

"Clay and I have our code words that I use to ask how he is doing with the porn and lust factor in his life. I think in my mind I believed that this accountability would bring a new and effective lifestyle of maintenance for him. But in my heart I wasn't prepared for what would come next. One night I could tell he seemed really low. He said he had slipped up and seen something on the computer. I was so upset. How could he tarnish MY clean house? I had my moment of anger and disappointment, but again, he was confessing again and sincerely asking me to forgive and pray for him.

"I knew from that moment on that trials would continue to come our way. I accepted the fact that I must never relax and think we had this problem beat. I resolved to pray often and hard for his purity of thought. In the name of Jesus I would ask God to keep smut far from Clay's eyes. I latched on to Proverbs 22:3 and prayed this verse over Clay as he slept: 'A prudent man foresees danger and takes precautions. The simpleton goes blindly on and suffers the consequences.' "

9. How can standing firm together create a powerful weapon against the enemy? We're there to pick each other up when we fall. How can you help your husband know that your love is there for him, even when he falls (See Ecclesiastes 4:9-10)?

EMBRACING THE TRUTH – 20 MINUTES

> **LEADER:** *This section focuses on helping group members integrate truths they've learned into their hearts and lives. Encourage and affirm group members for any gains they've made during this time of studying* Reclaiming Stolen Intimacy.

Marriage should never be taken lightly. God designed it to be a sacred union between a man and a woman. It's for a lifetime. God wants your life and your marriage to reflect His holiness and unity. Ephesians 5:31-32 explains: "A man will leave his father and mother and be united to his wife, and the two will become one flesh." This is a profound mystery—but I am talking about Christ and the church."

1. Do you really believe that marriage is a lifetime commitment no matter what? Will you pray and ask God to help you be wholeheartedly devoted to your husband? In the space below write your prayer to God.

It seems that we live in a world of disposable everything—including our marriages. If you're not happy, just get a divorce. If it ain't working for ya, move on. This is advice that the world throws at us. Think back to our little Crosse family motto: *Narrow or Wide*. Which path do you want to take for your life?

2. Think back on your wedding vows. Were you serious when you vowed to be there for your husband "for better or for worse?"

LETTER FROM A CONCERNED SISTER

"WOW! What an amazing testimony! I decided to read your book because my younger sister just discovered that her husband of four years is into pornography. As I read your book, I couldn't believe how similar your situations are. The feelings, the words that you said, all rang familiar as I listened to my sister talk about. So thank you for writing this and not letting pride keep this from helping so many. I have sent copies of your book to her and her husband and also to her pastor.

"Now for the hard part. My sister is a child of divorce. She has been advised to get a divorce and move on with her life as if this is an unforgivable offense. She filed papers yesterday, and I have not stopped crying. My husband and I have prayed and asked God to anoint your book as she reads it. We are also continuing to pray.

"Thank you again for coming out with this and for sticking with Clay through all of this. God has used your marriage mightily! We are called to be examples of Christ to a lost and dying world. Thank you for supplying the answers for those who are struggling with this issue. I wish you were able to duplicate yourself so that I could send one of you to my sister. It seems all of my godly advice gets drowned out by the worldly advice she's receiving. Even well-meaning Christians are giving advice contrary to what God would have for their lives. We must stay tuned in and squarely focused on God and His Word."

A Word from Renee

"Clay and I began to tell close friends and family about what was going on. Yes it was painful, but it helped to talk and receive support from the people closest to us. Some didn't have much to say, but some said just the right things. My grandmother told me she was proud that we were dealing with this head-on and that she knew God was going to use it to help others. She gave us some serious godly wisdom.

"I have to admit that I was very apprehensive about sharing what was going on in our lives. But, somewhere deep inside, I believed also that God was going to use this trial. And He continues to use it. We receive so many e-mails from people who are right where we were in 1998.

"There is no simple, quick fix for them. We tell them the same thing every time. Run to God! Turn to Him like you never have before. Dive into the Bible and pray. He is waiting to show Himself able to work a mighty work in your lives.

"Know that God may not be calling you to get up on a stage and shout to the world your struggle. But, you can be that voice to one other person whose path you cross. You will meet other couples going through the same thing.

"God can and will use you if you ask Him to help you be sensitive to others who are struggling. Your coming alongside them to support and encourage will be a lasting legacy of what God has done for your marriage."

Take heed to your spirit, and let none deal treacherously with the wife of his youth. For the Lord God of Israel says that He hates divorce, "for it covers one's garment with violence," says the Lord of hosts. Therefore take heed to your spirit, that you do not deal treacherously.

MALACHI 2:15-16, NIV

3. How badly do you want God to turn your shame into glory for your family legacy and in the lives of others who struggle with pornography and other marital issues?

4. Up the road, how might God be able to use what you are going through to help others? Is there someone God is putting on your heart that might be in a similar situation to the one you've faced? Let's pray about how you can reach out to them.

LEAVING A LEGACY

> *LEADER INSTRUCTIONS FOR THE GROUP EXPERIENCE: Bring a copy of the book,* The Power of a Praying Wife *by Stormie Omartian to the session. Give the women an opportunity to browse through it before or after the session.*

Would you be willing to pray this prayer from The Power of a Praying Wife for your marriage?"

"Lord, I pray You would protect our marriage from anything that would harm or destroy it. Shield it from our own selfishness and neglect, from the evil plans and desires of others, and from unhealthy or dangerous situations. May there be no thoughts of divorce or infidelity in our hearts, and none in our future. Set us free from past hurts, memories, and ties from previous relationships and unrealistic expectations of one another. I pray that there be no jealousy in either of us, or the low-self esteem that precedes that. Let nothing come into our hearts and habits that would threaten the marriage in any way, especially influences like alcohol, drugs, gambling, pornography, lust, or obsessions. Unite us in a bond of friendship, commitment, generosity, and understanding. Eliminate our immaturity, hostility, or feelings of inadequacy. Help us to make time for one another alone, to nurture and renew the marriage and remind ourselves of the reasons we were married in the first place. I pray that (husband's name) will be so committed to you, Lord, that his commitment to me will not waiver, no matter what storms come. I pray that our love for each other will grow stronger every day, so that we will never leave a legacy of divorce to our children." [2]

5. Examine the prayer again and fill in your own list of specific needs, along with your husband's name. Pray this prayer for your marriage.

6. **This is a pivotal question.** Are you solidly committed to your marriage? Are committed to leaving a legacy of God's grace and provision, not a legacy of divorce?

CONNECTING – 20 MINUTES

LEADER: *Use this final "Connecting" to launch group members as they continue on the healing and redemptive journey. Make yourself and other group members available for ongoing support. Consider exchanging e-mail addresses.*

YOU'VE GOT MAIL IN THE MAILBOX!

A WORD FROM A FRIEND

Dear Renee,

I wanted you to know that you have been constantly in my prayers and on my mind. God is up to something big. I can't wait to see how He gets the glory from this time of struggle and stretching. Here's a verse I read today: 'Finish what you started in me, God. Your love is eternal' (Psalm 138:8, The Message).

"This note meant so much to me. Talk about a good friend. A great friend! Yes, it took a moment out my friend's busy life to stop and write to me, but she cared and that's what means the most. I have saved that card for years, and it continues to be a source of encouragement in my life."

How are your card-writing skills? Let's dust them off. Several friends sent cards to me during my hardest days. Let me tell you, there is something special about seeing a card addressed to me waiting in the mailbox amidst the bills and credit card offers.

LEADER INSTRUCTIONS FOR THE GROUP EXPERIENCE: Provide some strips of paper—one for each group member. Bring a basket for the women to drop their strips of paper into once they have included their contact information.

Ask each member to write her name and address on a piece of paper and drop it into a basket. Then ask each member to take one. Urge the women to send a card to that person in the following days or weeks. Time will be required to write a note and put it in the mail, but the message is far greater than the words on the page.

MY ONGOING PRAYER NEEDS:

MY GROUP'S ONGOING PRAYER NEEDS:

GROUP NEXT STEPS

At the end of this *Reclaiming Stolen Intimacy* experience, group members will feel a close sense of connection. At the same time, they're aware that this is the final session. Depending upon your own plans for the group and/or the group views about continuing to meet and study another series, you need to be sensitive to what degree and sense of closure the group needs. Choose one or more of the following options...

OPTION 1: Suggest to the group that redemptive community has had time to take root in your meetings together. Remind them that their healing journeys are only beginning. Ask the group if they would consider staying together for continued support and redemption. Pass around 3 x 5" cards so people can jot down their potential interest. Other related recovery studies in the Picking Up the Pieces series include *Radical Reconciliation* (forgiveness) and *Redeeming the Tears* (dealing with losses and grief).

CONTINUED ...

OPTION 2: Encourage group members to join the next *Reclaiming Stolen Intimacy* group, either to go through the process again at a deeper level, or to take an active role in helping to lead the group as a mentor, small-group facilitator, accountability partner, or other job that fits well. (The group facilitator will try to fit people into the most suitable roles).

OPTION 3: If there are not enough to form a small group, refer the interested people to your pastor to connect them with an ongoing group. If you form a group that does not want to go through *Reclaiming Stolen Intimacy* again, we suggest your next step would be to go through the Serendipity House study entitled *Great Beginnings*. You may order this and other group resources online at www.SerendipityHouse.com.

OPTION 4: Some groups like to meet each month or so for a get-together at a restaurant. You may consider this. Knowing a reunion is not far off may help group members with this study's wrap-up, especially if you don't plan to continue meeting as a group.

Taking It Home

"Someday" Journal

It's time to determine how you want your "someday" to look. I'm talking about legacy living. Write to God and tell Him what you most want for your life, how you want your family and friends to remember you. Most of all, what do you want God to say to you someday?

Spend some time writing your own legacy letter or prayer to share with your family. Look toward the future believing God will continue to do a mighty work in your life, your husband's life, and the lives of your children. Nothing is impossible with Him.

Take this verse to heart:
Ah, Sovereign Lord, you have made the heavens and earth by your great power and outstretched arm. Nothing is too hard for you.
JEREMIAH 32:17, NIV

God didn't do a healing and restorative work exclusively for Clay and Renee. He stands ready to work in your life too. God didn't just restore what we had; He's given us so much more than we could have asked or imagined as we persevered through the pain—as we took the narrow path.

SOMEDAY ...

NOTES:

1. William F. Harley Jr., *His Needs, Her Needs* (Grand Rapids, MI: Revell, 2001).

2. Stormie Omartian, *The Power of a Praying Wife* (Eugene, OR: Harvest House Publishers, 1997).

Required Supplies and Preparation for Each Session

This section lists the supplies required for the Group Experiences in each session of the study. Detailed procedural instructions for the experiences are given within each session.

Session 1:

Supplies:
- 3 x 5 index cards or blank sheets of paper for each group member + pens
- CD player/MP3 + CD *Run the Earth, Watch the Skies* or downloaded song "Untitled Hymn: Come to Jesus"

Preparation:
Review the "Group Covenant" on page 21 prior to the first group session.

Session 2:

Supplies:
- Magazines on variety of topics (home improvement, gardening, fashion, etc.)
- 3 x 5 index cards or blank sheets of paper for each group member + pens
- CD player + CD *Somebody's Daughter* from Serendipity
- Large tear sheets or poster boards for 3 subgroups

Preparation:
Review again the "Group Covenant" on page 21 prior to the second group session. Prepare to review this and have each group member sign it during the session.

Session 3:

Supplies:
- Gather a variety of objects to create an obstacle course
- One blindfold
- Stakes and white ribbon for each group member + one or two hammers
- CD/MP3 player + CD *David—Ordinary Man—Extraordinary Man* or downloaded song "When I Am Afraid" by Clay Crosse

Preparation:
Scatter objects on the floor to make a small obstacle course. Also bring a blindfold. If time allows, repeat the minefield activity with another pair.

Session 4:

Supplies:
- DVD player and TV + DVD from the Survivor TV series at a video store or watch clips online at www.cbs.com/primetime/survivor16
- CD/MP3 player + CD *Live and the Door* or downloaded song "Legacy" by Nichole Nordeman
- 3 x 5 index cards for each woman to take home. See "Taking It Home" notes

Session 5:

Supplies: - Extra 3 x 5 index cards
- CD/MP3 player + CD *Lifesong* or downloaded song "Praise You in This Storm" by Casting Crowns

Session 6:

Supplies: - Rose or other flower in a vase for display
- The *Secret Seductress* (Serendipity); *Shattered Vows* by Debra Laaser; *The Seven Desires of Every Heart* by Mark and Debra Laaser (Zondervan)
- CD/MP3 player + CD *Relentless* or downloaded song "In Better Hands" by Natalie Grant

Preparation:

Bring a copy of the 3 books prior to session 6. Encourage group members to pick up powerful healing study *The Secret Seductress* for their husbands. *Shattered Vows* is a good book geared to women. *The Seven Desires of Every Heart* is an excellent book for men and women.

Session 7:

Supplies: - You may want to get a copy of the book *Power of a Praying Wife* by Stormie Omartian to display in the session, or pick up a copy for each group member if you have the budget.

Session 8:

Supplies: - 3x5-inch note cards and pens for each group member
- CD/MP3 player + CD *Awakening, Vol. 1,* presented by Christ Community Church or downloaded song "Jesus I Am Resting, Resting"
- Strips of paper—one for each group member. Bring a basket to drop the strips of paper into once group members note their contact information.

Preparation:

Bring a copy of the book, *The Power of a Praying Wife* by Stormie Omartian to the session. Give the women an opportunity to browse through it before or after the group session.

Review the "Group Next Steps" on pages 118-119 prior to the final meeting.

Leading a Successful Recovery Group

You need to accept the limitations of leadership. You cannot transform a life. You must lead your group to the Bible, the Holy Spirit, and the power of Christian community. By doing so your group will have all the tools necessary to walk through the healing journey and embrace life and hope on the other side. The journey must extend well beyond this study. But the experience will allow your group members to move toward wholeness.

Make the following things available at each session

- *Beyond the Shadows* book for each attendee
- Bible for each attendee
- Boxes of tissue
- Snacks and refreshments plus dark chocolates (calming properties)
- Pens or pencils for each attendee

NOTE: Every session requires other supplies for the group experiences that greatly enhance the healing journey. Check the supplies list and be sure you gather what's needed in each session.

The Setting

General Tips:

1. Prepare for each meeting by reviewing the material, praying for each group member, asking the Holy Spirit to join you, and making Jesus the centerpiece of every experience.

2. Create the right environment by making sure chairs are arranged so each person can see the eyes of every other attendee. Set the room temperature at 69 degrees. If meeting in a home, make sure pets are in a location where they cannot interrupt the meeting. Request that cell phones are turned off unless someone is expecting an emergency call. Have music playing as people arrive (volume low enough for people to converse) and, if possible, burn a sweet-smelling candle.

3. Try to have soft drinks and coffee available for early arrivals.

4. Have someone with the spiritual gift of hospitality ready to make any new attendees feel welcome.

5. Be sure there is adequate lighting so that everyone can read without straining.

6. There are four types of questions used in each session: Observation (What is the passage telling us?), Interpretation (What does the passage mean?), Self-revelation (How am I doing in light of the truth unveiled?), and Application (Now that I know what I know, what will I do to integrate this truth into my life?). You may not have time to use all the questions in each session, but be sure to use some from each of these types of questions.

7. Connect with group members away from group time. The amount of participation you'll receive from group member during meetings is directly related to the amount of time that you connect with them away from the meetings.

8. Don't get impatient about the depth of relationship group members are experiencing. Building real Christian Community takes time.

9. Be sure pens and/or pencils are available for attendees at each meeting.

10. Never ask someone to pray aloud without first getting their permission. Ask for volunteers to help with various aspects of the group, including reading aloud.

Every Meeting:

1. Before the connecting time, do not say, "Now we're going to do connecting." The meeting should feel like a conversation from beginning to end, not a classroom experience.

2. Be certain every member responds to the "Getting Started" questions. The goal is for every person to hear his own voice early in the meeting. People will then feel comfortable to converse later on. If group members can't think of a response, let them know you'll come back to them after the others have spoken.

3. Remember, a great group leader talks less than 10% of the time. If you ask a question and no one answers, just wait. If you create an environment where you fill the gaps of silence, the group will quickly learn they needn't join you in the conversation.

4. Don't be hesitant to call people by name as you ask them to respond to questions or to give their opinions. Be sensitive, but engage everyone in the conversation.

5. Don't ask people to read aloud unless you have gotten their permission prior to the meeting. Feel free to ask for volunteers to read.

The Group

Every group is made up of a unique set of personalities, backgrounds, and life experiences. This diversity creates a dynamic distinctive for each group. Embracing the unique character of your group and its individuals is vital to a deep healing experience.

Treat each person as special, responsible, and valuable members of this Christian community. By doing so you'll bring out the best in each of them thus creating a living, breathing, life-changing group dynamic.

What Can You Expect?

Because group members are still experiencing and emotions are stirring within them, at the outset, members will be on their best behavior. Some attendees will, as they understand the openness necessary and requested by the group, withdraw for at time.

Some attendees will experience fatigue which will lead to them shutting down emotionally. This is natural and is one of the things our body does to prevent overload.

There are emotions and phases unique to people dealing with depression and anxiety. These will be addressed as the group progresses through the healing journey. Be sensitive.

You will be the most helpful when you focus on how each individual is adjusting and reminding them that hurt, anger , and other emotions are normal and extremely helpful to understand and express on the path to healing..

If there's severe depression, or short tempers, changes in physical habits, such as sleep, eating, apathy, and others appear to be long term, refer people to a pastor or competent Christian counselor. **You can get a list of counselors from your pastor or www.aacc.net.**

Places may also bring back memories or temptations that are difficult to deal with alone. If a member has an engagement in a location that would be a painful reminder of the past go with them and/or ask the group members if one of them might be there for this individual. You may hear, "This is something I have to do alone." You can respect this desire, but remind them that it's God who will give them strength, and that you will pray.

WHAT CAN YOU DO?

Support – Provide plenty of time for support among the group members. Encourage members to connect with each other between meetings. It's very important that you help each person in the group to develop a strong, supportive accountability group

Shared Feelings – Reassure the members how normal their feelings are; even if relief and sadness are mixed together. Encourage the members to share their feelings with one another.

Advice Giving – Encourage cross-talk (members talking to each other), but limit advice giving. "Should" and "ought to" statements tend to increase the guilt and shame.

Silence – Silence is not a problem. Even though it may seem awkward, silence is just a sign that people are not ready to talk. It DOES NOT mean they aren't thinking or feeling. If the silence needs to be broken, be sure you break it with the desire to move forward.

Prayer – Prayer is vital to healing. Starting and ending with prayer is important. However, people may need prayer in the middle of the session. If a member is sharing and you sense a need to pray, then begin to look for a place to add it.

Feelings vs. Right Choices and Thinking – There may be a temptation to overemphasize feelings rather that choices and thinking. It is important that you encourage the group to keep moving forward regardless of how we feel. Processing emotions is a vital aspect of the healing journey, but left to feelings alone, progress will shut down.

As you move toward the end of the study, be aware that it is a bittersweet time for the group. It will be painful for them to say goodbye to one another. Set a time for the group to have a reunion.

Group Meeting Structure

Each of your group meetings will include a four-part agenda.

1. Getting Started:

This section includes fun, uplifting questions to kick off each session and help group members get to know one another better, as they begin the journey of becoming a connected community. These questions prepare the group for meaningful discussion throughout the session.

2. Discovering the Truth:

The heart of each session is the interactive Bible study time. The goal is for the group to discover biblical truths through open, discovery questions that lead to further investigation. The emphasis in this section is two-fold:
(1) to provide instruction about the process of recovery and freedom; and
(2) understand what the Bible says through interaction within your group.

NOTE: To help the group experience a greater sense of community, it is important for everybody to participate in the "Discovering the Truth" and "Embracing the Truth" discussions. Even though people in a group have differing levels of biblical knowledge, it is vital that group members encourage one another share what they are observing, thinking, and feeling about the Bible passages.

3. Embracing the Truth:

All study should direct group members to action and life change. This section continues the Bible study time, but with an emphasis on leading group members toward integrating the truths they have discovered into their lives. The questions are very practical and application-focused.

4. Connecting:

One of the key goals of this study is to lead group members to grow closer to one another as the group develops a sense of community. This section focuses on connecting with God, with others, and with your heart. There are also opportunities for encouraging, supporting, and praying for one another.

Taking it Home:

Between each session, there is some homework for group members. This includes a question to take to God or a question to take to the heart, and typically a task to help prepare for the next session. **These experiences are a critical part of your journey of healing and freedom.**

ABOUT THE AUTHORS

Renee and Clay Crosse speak at various seminars and conferences nationwide promoting the message of their ministry, Holy Homes. Clay also has an extensive concert and worship leading schedule. He is a three-time Dove Award winner including the 1994 New Artist of the year. He has had nine Number 1 songs including "I Surrender All," "He Walked a Mile" and "I Will Follow Christ." Clay and Renee coauthored *I Surrender All: Rebuilding a Marriage Broken by Pornography*. Each has another book coming out soon.

The Crosses reside in Memphis, Tennessee with their four children, Shelby, Savannah, Garrett (adopted from China in 2007), and Sophie (adopted from China in 2005).

For more information about Holy Homes or to schedule the Crosses for marriage conferences, youth conferences, worship services, or concerts, visit www.HolyHomes.org.

ACKNOWLEDGMENTS

This project was a true team effort. We wish to thank the team that labored alongside us to make this life-changing small-group experience a reality.

Managing Director: Ron Keck
Women's Ministry Director: Pamela Case
Supporting Writer: Ben Colter
Editorial Team: Saundria Keck, Ben Colter, Carolyn Gregory, Jessie Weaver
Art Director: Darin Clark
Cover Designer: Brian Marschall (www.MarschallArts.com)
Production Designer: Joe Moore of Powell Creative Inc.

GROUP DIRECTORY

Write your name on this page. Pass your books around and ask your group members to fill in their names and contact information in each other's books.

Your Name: _____

Name: _____   Name: _____
Address: _____   Address: _____
City: _____   City: _____
Zip Code: _____   Zip Code: _____
Home Phone: _____   Home Phone: _____
Mobile Phone: _____   Mobile Phone: _____
E-mail: _____   E-mail: _____

Name: _____   Name: _____
Address: _____   Address: _____
City: _____   City: _____
Zip Code: _____   Zip Code: _____
Home Phone: _____   Home Phone: _____
Mobile Phone: _____   Mobile Phone: _____
E-mail: _____   E-mail: _____

Name: _____   Name: _____
Address: _____   Address: _____
City: _____   City: _____
Zip Code: _____   Zip Code: _____
Home Phone: _____   Home Phone: _____
Mobile Phone: _____   Mobile Phone: _____
E-mail: _____   E-mail: _____

Name: _____   Name: _____
Address: _____   Address: _____
City: _____   City: _____
Zip Code: _____   Zip Code: _____
Home Phone: _____   Home Phone: _____
Mobile Phone: _____   Mobile Phone: _____
E-mail: _____   E-mail: _____

Name: _____   Name: _____
Address: _____   Address: _____
City: _____   City: _____
Zip Code: _____   Zip Code: _____
Home Phone: _____   Home Phone: _____
Mobile Phone: _____   Mobile Phone: _____
E-mail: _____   E-mail: _____